PAINT RECIPES

PAINT

Original photography by
Marie-Louise Avery and Sue Baker

JOCASTA INNES AROUND THE HOUSE

RECIPES

Text by SARAH DELAFIELD COOK

MACMILLAN

AROUND THE HOUSE is intended as a series that will expand into a whole shelf of stylish, practical and focussed handbooks for home decorators. Small enough to be affordable, but long enough to deal with their subjects in depth, they will offer a generous choice of hands-on projects, clearly explained and amplified by excellent, specially-commissioned photographs. If cooks can buy small, subject-specific books such as Pasta, Soups and Salads, why shouldn't decorators be offered the same approach, and choice?

I believe this series – something of a publishing 'first' – will encourage a radical re-think of decorating books, their treatment, format and presentation.

Watch this space!

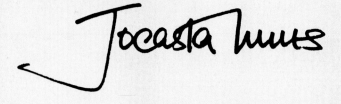

CONTENTS

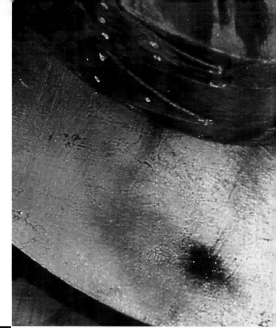

INTRODUCTION

The aim of this book is to enable you to take full advantage of the potential of paint. It introduces you to some of the many ways in which paint can be used and looks at the basics of these techniques. For it is only through understanding materials and how and why they function that you will achieve successful and satisfying finishes. This is why we start by examining the origins of paint and its essential ingredients. We describe traditional raw materials and compare them to modern-day equivalents, look at mixing procedures and see how varying proportions of ingredients produce different paints for different purposes.

In Section Two there are seven classic recipes for the home decorator, in which traditional and modern ingredients are combined to make paints for every purpose. When you have worked through these you will have grasped the fundamentals of paint and glaze mixing, and be well equipped to take on most decorative projects. However, this book is not made up only of recipes based on raw materials: in Sections Three, Four and Five many of the techniques make use of ready-made products. We use the word 'recipe' to refer to an overall theme, to imply a combination of different parts, whether special ingredients, a sequence of applications or innovative combinations of equipment.

The opportunities that paint provides are endless – and thrilling. It transforms surfaces rapidly and effectively, it can unify and harmonize an interior, give richness to a room, create moods, add elegance and refinement. Above all, it can express your individuality. Practise and play with ingredients, have fun – all recipes can be adapted, that is the sign of a confident paint 'chef' – but get to know the materials first. There will then be no limitation on your decorative ambitions. You will be in control; you will be the paint magician.

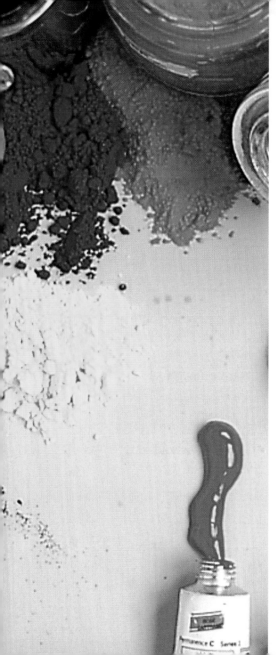

GENERAL PRINCIPLES
FOR A PAINT CHEF

The more familiar you are
with paint ingredients, the more
confident you will be working with
the materials and achieving the final
finish, whether it be transforming a
mundane object like a battered
mirror, bringing light and space into
a dark basement room or giving
new life to old bathroom tiles.

A basic principle for paint chefs is that, as with all recipes, whether you are mixing a cocktail, baking a soufflé – or creating an antiquing glaze – the proportions of ingredients are all-important. If the ratio is incorrect you may create a very different mixture and arrive at a very different result. You may reduce the paint's ability to adhere to the surface, its efficiency in retaining a pattern or its durability. This is why it is important to appreciate the nature of each ingredient and follow recipes faithfully when you start. Once you have learnt how ingredients react to each other and how this determines the final effect, you can begin to experiment. Skilled craftsmen often digress from the 'book' and create their own 'personalized' recipes with added extras, and this is certainly the sign of a confident paint chef. You, too, will be able to do this, but only when you know your ingredients.

WHAT IS PAINT?

Paint is essentially made of three main ingredients: a binder, a tinting agent and a solvent. Colour needs to be bound by something to make it stick to a surface, hence the binder. In turn, the binder needs something that will allow it to be applied, that gives it flexibility and fluidity, hence the solvent. Once these ingredients are combined, the result is a material that provides colour, protection and decoration.

Commercial production Commercially manufactured paints go through a long and complicated process that involves many testing stages, as characteristics like viscosity and colour are adjusted. However, the method is essentially the one that you would use at home – although yours is much more simplified version.

Binders Binders provide the main 'body' of paint and hold the ingredients together, suspending both tinting agent and solvent. The choice of binder depends on the amount of paint needed and the surface to be coated. Traditionally, decorators used 'found' materials like chalk, lime or milk solids for water-based paints and natural organic oils for oil colours. Materials more commonly associated with the kitchen – egg yolk and egg white are examples – were used to create durable paints for fine work. Binders for glazes – transparent paints that are brushed out thinly over a base coat which remains clearly visible – were 'sticky' materials like beer and vinegar (see pages 70 and 92 for traditional glaze recipes). The high sugar content of beer enables it to hold and suspend colour and, because it is extremely fluid, the glazes it creates are exceptionally delicate and transparent. Vinegar holds pigment in suspension in much the same way. It was probably first used for graining in nineteenth century America when country craftsmen devised a method of imitating woodgrain with cheaper materials than those used by master grainers.

Nowadays commercial manufacturers concentrate on producing mainly water-based acrylic products that are held together by synthetic, man-made binders known as acrylic polymers. These work by forming a thin film on the surface of the paint and allow it to be washed down more easily, but they do give the final finish a more synthetic, plastic appearance. Additional binders are sometimes used to thicken the paint, extend it, add texture or alter its drying time.

Ready-made paints are useful binders. They can be tinted further to make new shades, diluted with solvent to create transparency, or a ready-made glaze can be added to them to extend the 'open' or workable time. They offer a short cut. If you are creating a dark colour, for instance, it will be quicker and more economical to add a tinting agent to a ready-mixed shade rather than start with a white paint.

Binders for water and oil-based paints and glazes

1 Linseed oil The traditional binding ingredient for oil paint, extracted from the flax plant

2 Lime putty Lime, dug from the earth and 'slaked' (added to water) makes up the bulk of limewash, a thin, watery paint that hardens when exposed to air, and with several layers builds up an opacity but softness of colour

3 Whiting, or chalk, has been used for centuries for tradtional distemper. Its chalky, powdery texture gives pastel shades a unique 'pearly' bloom

4 Acrylic scumble glaze A modern, ready-mixed medium made from synthetic polymers to which artist's acrylic colours and water is added to make up water-based glazes

5 Oil-based scumble glaze A modern, ready-mixed oil-based medium made from linseed oil, driers and resins to which artist's oil colours and solvent (white spirit) is added

6 Egg has long been used as a binder in finer paints, such as egg tempera, for delicate handwork and fine art

7 Animal glue Rabbit skin and other glues have been used for centuries to bind bulky, water-based paints such as distemper. Melt in hot water, and add slowly to the ingredients. As it is organic, discard excess after use to prevent decay

8 Polyvinyl acrylic (PVA) A modern glue, used for binding water-based paints and glazes. Use also as a sealer and strong adhesive

9 Gum arabic Naturally-produced and water-soluble, available as liquid or crystal; most commonly used to bind finer paints like gouache and watercolour

Traditional binders	Use
Whiting (chalk)	Distemper (interior walls and ceilings)
Lime	Limewash (interior and exterior walls)
Casein (non-fat milk solids)	Milk paint (interior walls and fine work)
Oil	Oil paint (woodwork and fine art)
Animal or vegetable glues	Chalky paint; watercolours (fine art)
Egg yolk (with added casein)	Egg tempera (fine art)

Contemporary binders	
Acrylic polymers	Emulsion paint (interior and exterior walls)
Polyvinyl acetate (PVA)	Synthetic glue (binds paint)
Oil scumble glaze	Tinted to make glazes for special effects
Acrylic scumble glaze	Tinted to make glazes for special effects

Other ready-mixed materials can be used as binders. Oil and acrylic scumble glazes – designed to hold tinting agent and solvent in a transparent glaze – are widely available. These transparent binders are slow drying and so are used for special effects such as ragging, marbling and woodgraining. Oil-based scumbles are made from linseed oil, driers and resins (a recipe for one is one page 54; acrylic scumbles from acrylic resin.

Varnishes and shellacs both hold and suspend colour and can be used to bind ingredients. For example, a home-made lacquer paint (page 50) can be created by mixing pigment into shellac, a glossy, fast drying plant resin. Some paints are held together with glue: gum arabic, obtained from trees, binds the pigments in water-colours, and the binder in distemper, a traditional wall paint, is rabbit skin glue.

Tinting agent The tinting agent is the second main ingredient of a paint or glaze. A huge variety of materials is now available in tubes and bottles but traditionally only pure pigments were added to a binder. Pigments come in powder form, ground to a super-fine consistency, and are obtained from the earth, from plant matter or from mineral deposits. Typically, earth pigments are named after their place of origin; colours such as raw sienna and burnt umber come from Sienna and Umbria in Italy. Mineral pigments provide the brighter shades such as viridian, ultramarine blue and cadmium yellow. Some have been discovered comparatively recently; cadmium, for instance, a toxic, silvery metal which produces a wide range of pigments within the red and yellow band of the colour spectrum, was found in zinc mines in about 1817. Pigments obtained from plants, or from resins exuded by them, are closer to dyes as they dissolve completely in the binder. Typical colours are rose madder, turmeric and indigo.

Pigments are useful as they can be added to both water- and oil-based binders. The colour they provide is intense because it is pure, not 'padded out' with fillers, and a little goes a long way. Pigments are not standardized so colours vary subtly from supplier to supplier; this should be seen as providing interesting variations rather than as a problem.

Artist's paints are ready-made colours that contain a high level of pigment. They are packaged in small quantities, usually tubes or small pots, and are expensive compared to decorator's paints. They are available as water-based acrylics or oils and should only be mixed with binders that use the corresponding solvent. Oils tend to be richer and creamier than acrylics and stay wet for much longer. Acrylics are more plastic and quick drying; it is easier to waste them as, once squeezed out, they 'film over' and dry hard. Gouache, another concentrated artist's colour, is watercolour

Tinting agents and solvents for water- and oil-based paints and glazes

Tinting agents come in many forms. Traditionally, **earth and mineral pigments**, 1, have been used to provide the colour for paints and glazes. Obtained from natural deposits or plant matter, these are ground to a fine powder with a mortar and pestle, with solvent added to make a paste. **Bronze powders**, 2, also ground finely, can be added to binders to make shimmering metallic paints and glazes. Nowadays, **artist's tube colours**, 3, are more commonly used for tinting. Both acrylic and oil provide intense, concentrated colour in an easy-to-use form. **Gouache**, 4, and **water-colour**, 5, tend to be used for fine art rather than for tinting bulkier mediums, as they are finer and come in smaller quantities. The most commonly-used solvent in decorative painting is **water**, for water-based and acrylic products, **white spirit** (a substitute for turpentine) for oil-based products, and **methylated spirit** for alcohol-based products, 6.

Traditional tinting agents	Contemporary tinting agents
Earth pigments	Artist's oil colours
Mineral pigments	Artist's acrylic colours
Plant pigments	Artist's gouache colours; universal stainer; poster paint; student's ranges

bound with gum arabic; chalk is added to make it more opaque. It is usually available only in small tubes so may be uneconomical.

Universal stainers can be added to both water- and oil-based binders. They are very strong, highly concentrated colours and go a long way. However, their colour range tends to be limited and the shades are quite crude. Other, cheaper, tinting agents are poster paints and 'student' ranges which contain less pigment and more extenders than other colours and so are less pure. They are available in larger packs and are adequate for home-made paints. However, you will have to use more of them for a particularly deep shade.

Solvents Solvents are the third chief ingredient of paints and glazes. They dilute the main body of the paint and the tinting agent and make the mixture fluid and manageable. Turpentine or today's cheaper and more widely available equivalent, white spirit, is the solvent for oil-based paints and varnishes, methylated spirits is used for alcohol-based lacquers and shellacs, and water for water-based and acrylic products. Solvents are important in that they create transparency in glazes and washes and extend open times. They are also used to wipe away mistakes and to clean brushes and equipment.

Their reaction to certain binders is utilized in some finishes. On page 76, for example, our shagreen finish is produced by spraying water onto a wet oil-based glaze so that tiny circles open up. On page 98 we imitate fossil stone by using both white spirit and methylated spirits to create different dispersal effects on a multi-coloured, wet, oil-based glaze.

Solvent	Materials and uses
Water	All water-based and acrylic paints, e.g. emulsion paints, artist's acrylic colours; acrylic scumble glazes and varnishes; traditional paints and glazes, e.g. distemper, limewash, casein paints, beer and vinegar glazes.
White spirit	All oil-based products including scumble glazes, undercoats, eggshell and gloss paints, varnishes, waxes.
Methylated spirits	All shellac-based products, e.g. button polish, white polish, French polish.

Additional ingredients Additional ingredients in many modern paints have improved their quality, making them more stable and lengthening their shelf life. A typical white matt emulsion paint, for example, contains biocide to guard against bacteria and act as a preservative, defoamer to keep the material stable and prevent frothing, pH buffer to neutralize the different components, and numerous other ingredients like coalescents and dispersants.

TYPES OF PAINT

Historically, simple or crude colours were made in the home or on the farm with local materials. Finer paints like the concentrated oils needed by artists and craftsmen were made in workshops with more expensive or rare ingredients. Commercial products first came on the market in the late eighteenth century and it was the 1920s before manufactured paints became widely available. Today there is huge competition within the industry to produce leading-edge products and a vast range to choose from.

Water-based paints Traditionally, most wall effects were achieved with soft, water-based mixtures. Materials like chalk, lime or milk solids were mixed with water and tinted with pure pigments to make cheap, household paints. Distemper (see page 44) is a classic, chalk-based example that has been used for centuries across the world. Chalk (whiting) was dug from local pits, crushed to powder and bound with pigment in an animal glue and water medium. Limewash, another traditional water-based paint, used lime putty as its main constituent and was favoured for its disinfectant properties – hence its frequent use in cellars, stables, larders and kitchens. Distemper and limewash both have a chalky, matt finish which is permeable, allowing walls to 'breathe'. In recent years there has been a vogue for these traditional, 'authentic' paints, particularly among conservationists, and they certainly have a texture and luminosity that is missing from modern, synthetic products. However, they do tend to be less durable. Soft distemper, for instance cannot be washed down, but nor should it be varnished.

Contemporary water-based products, more commonly known as emulsions, vinyls or latex, are made of synthetic acrylic resins and polymers. They create a thin

Water-based paint	Type and use
Distemper	Traditional wall paint made from chalk, rabbit skin glue, water and pigment. Very dense, powdery, usually pastel shades. Cannot be washed.
Limewash	Traditional wall paint made from lime putty, water and pigment; antibacterial properties. Applied over lime or gypsum plaster in thin washes or over wood for a silvery bloom. Hardens when exposed to air. Durable, ages beautifully. Casein is sometimes added for extra durability.
Acrylic primer or convertor	Good, all-purpose primer for walls and woodwork made from acrylic polymers; also useful for priming laminated surfaces such as melamine and Formica. Available in white. Not as thick as oil-based undercoat.
Emulsion paint	Standard, modern-day paint for interior walls made from acrylic polymers and polyvinyl acetate (PVA) combined and dispersed in water to form an emulsion binder. Quick drying, available in matt or vinyl silk (see below). Not suitable for glaze work. Can be washed. Available in very thick, one-coat versions.
Vinyl silk (see above)	Unabsorbent so can be a used for glaze work. Higher content of PVA gives sheen. Quick drying but tends to be very thin, so more coats required. Can be washed and is tougher than matt emulsion.
Acrylic eggshell	Water-based version of traditional oil-based eggshell (see page 26). Suitable for wood work. Very dense and sticky; dries to a soft sheen that is hard and very durable. Ideal as a base for oil and acrylic scumble glazes. May retain brushmarks.
Acrylic gloss	Relatively new paint, suitable for woodwork Dries to a hard- wearing, glossy finish but is not as smooth as oil-based gloss (see page 26; brushmarks do not level out as well as with oils.
Impasto or textured paint	Contemporary paint to create texture on walls; an emulsion with added thickener and binder. Dries to a matt, chalky texture ideal for colour washing, sanding to give a distressed look.
Woodwash	Specialist paint available from Paint Magic. Chalky, matt and opaque with added thickeners; can be burnished with wire wool and polished with wax to create a deep shine or diluted to use as a woodstain.

A diluted distemper washed over a solid coat makes a vibrant, animated wall finish.

film over the surface of the paint and dry to an opaque, perfectly smooth, uniform finish. Unlike their predecessors they do not allow walls to 'breathe' and often contribute to problems like damp, a common complaint, by sealing moisture within them. These water-based paints are available in various finishes – matt, vinyl silk, eggshell and, more recently, gloss – which have varying levels of durability: the more acrylic resins they contain, the more shiny and durable the finish, hence the use of acrylic eggshell paints on woodwork and furniture.

Water-based paints are quick drying, they do not contain harmful solvents that require rooms to be ventilated or any special safety measures, and equipment is easily cleaned in water. Some disadvantages are that they are a little less durable than oil-based products; and their quicker drying time makes it more difficult for beginners to execute specialist finishes, particularly 'subtractive' effects like sponging-off colour. However, the industry looks set to improve the range year by year and it is foreseeable that oil-based paints will soon become a thing of the past.

Oil-based paints Oil-based paints were first used in the sixteenth century. Although ceilings and exterior walls were painted, as always, with water-based distempers and limewashes, oil colours were used for interior walls in wealthier households. This was very much linked with the fashion for cladding walls in wooden panels. For most of the sixteenth century these were made from hardwoods and left bare but, during the seventeenth, interior fashion moved away from these heavy tones to lighter shades and the panelling was painted. This was particularly popular during the rococo period of the eighteenth century when salons were fitted out in fine panels with delicate moulding and carved decoration painted in pale, feminine tones: soft greys, blues, greens and off-whites.

Traditional oil paint is a mixture of vegetable oil, pigment and driers. A variety of oils, including poppy and walnut, was used, but raw linseed oil, obtained from the seeds of the flax plant, was the most common and used to make decorator's paints. The seeds were ground and the resulting oil allowed to mature over several months; bleaching and boiling the oil helped the paint to dry more quickly be more durable. Cold pressing produced a finer quality product, used to make artist's oil colours; pigments were crushed and ground in a pestle and mortar, then mixed into the oil on a marble slab with a palette knife. Driers, also known as siccative or metallic salts, were added to accelerate the drying process, and resins added if a glossy finish was wanted.

Paints

1 Colourwash
Water-based, ready-mixed glazes are now readily available for creating 'broken' colour effects for walls

2 Matt emulsion (latex)
Interior and exterior emulsions are improving in quality and colour range each year; look for simple, flat emulsions in historic colours

3 Flat oil
Rarely used now, but a paint of exceptional rich-ness and opacity

4 Oil-based gloss
Much the toughest and most hardwearing paint for woodwork

5 Acrylic eggshell
Water-based satin finish eggshells for woodwork are now used almost as much as oil-based ones, though with a less smooth finish

6, 7 Woodwash and woodwash stain
A popular specialist, custom-made paint; Paint Magic Woodwash enables a range of effects from washing to burnishing

8 **9**

10

11

8, 9 Distemper
The chalkiness and
'breathing qualities' of this
traditional paint make it
ideal for cottages and
other older buildings

10, 11 Limewash
Made from lime putty,
water and pigment, and
here shown in several
shades, limewash is
applied in a series of thin
layers to exterior and
exterior walls

Paint	**Type and use**
Undercoat	Thick, sticky, white primer for woodwork; also adheres well to plastic and metal. Flat, slightly chalky texture. Thick, opaque coverage fills small indentations in surface; can be tinted; good for adding to oil-based scumble glaze to make it more opaque and 'knock back' intense colours.
Red oxide metal primer	Dark red primer ideal for protecting metals from rust before decoration.
Flat oil	A specialist paint, used on interior walls. Extra-matt. Shows scuff marks but looks very sophisticated.
Lead paint	Highly toxic paint for walls and woodwork, no longer on the market for interior use, although it is sometimes available for the restoration of Grade I listed houses. Flat and chalky. Supremely protective.
Eggshell	Great favourite for woodwork like skirtings and window frames; also used as a base for oil glazes and for mixing into glazes. More fashionable apearance than gloss; dull sheen and tough, opaque coverage. Dries slowly and must be applied smoothly.
Gloss	Very durable, hard-wearing paint, good for kitchen splashbacks that need a lot of wiping, woodwork and metal furniture. High level of resin gives deep, gloss finish. Before gloss was invented, flat oils were varnished to achieve the look. Good surface preparation needed as gloss will highlight any unevenness in the surface.
Japan paint	Originated in nineteenth-century attempt to imitate Japanese lacquer. Suitable for metal and primed woodwork, decorative painting like inn signs. High opacity; dries glossy and hard.
Metal paint	Made from resins, heat-hardened glass and pigments. Quick drying, extremely hard-wearing. Brushes require special cleaner.
Enamel paint	High-gloss paint suitable for metal, primed woodwork. Originated in the nineteenth century from a mixture of varnish and oil. Ingredients are ground to a super-fine quality to produce smoothness and high gloss.
Floor paint	High proportion of varnish makes it hard-wearing and water-resistant.

Today oil-based paints are most commonly used on woodwork, particularly soft woods like pine which require more protection than hard woods. Their advantages are that they are more flexible and durable than water-based products, their texture is richer and more velvety and because they take longer to dry there is more time to create difficult special effects like marbling. Their down side is that they contain flammable and toxic solvents – white spirit or paint thinners – and rooms must be ventilated when you work with them.

WAXES, VARNISHES AND LACQUERS

These materials are not essentially part of the paint family but they play an important role in decorative paint techniques. Although they are usually classed as finishing products, they can also be used as mediums for particular effects or catalysts for specific reactions. These are illustrated overleaf – look carefully and appreciate the differences.

Wax comes in many forms and from a variety of sources, and is classed as oil-based because its solvent is turpentine or white spirit. It protects and waterproofs bare wood, leaving it with a rich, smooth patina, and can be used as a soft, texturing medium. Pigments or bronze powders can be mixed into wax that has been softened with heat and applied to moulded surfaces to produce intriguing finishes (see page 81 for our antique bronze effect). Wax can also be softened and mixed with pigment diluted in a little white spirit, to create subtle shades that both protect and colour wood and painted surfaces.

Historically, varnishes were made from tree gums and resins. Mixed with oils they became insoluble in water, producing a resistant, waterproof coating for painted and unpainted surfaces. A disadvantage of these traditional varnishes is that they

Waxes, varnishes, lacquers and other finishes

1 Dead flat varnish

2 Eggshell (satin finish) varnish

3 Gloss varnish

4 White polish shellac

5 Button polish shellac

6 Craquelure

7 Gilt wax

8 Colourwax

9 Crackleglaze

10 Dutch metal gilding

11 Boot polish

12 Distressing

10

11

12

tend to yellow with time because of their high oil content and this alters the colour of the underlying surface. Acrylic alternatives that do not do this are now available; they are totally colourless and also dry very quickly. However, they tend to be brittle and are certainly less sensuous to the touch. As with all acrylic products, brushmarks do not dissolve out as well as they do with oils. Varnishes can be used as media in which to suspend colour and are particularly useful for mixing quick antiquing glazes.

Shellacs are extra-thin, transparent, alcohol-based solutions derived from a secretion of the 'lac' beetle. Dark brown in colour, this is collected and stored in the form of flakes which are dissolved in methylated spirits to make a resinous, fast-drying, glossy spirit varnish. Shellac should not be confused with genuine lacquer which is derived from the sap of the 'lac' tree and is one of the hardest materials known to man. There are different grades of shellac. Some, like button polish, are heated to produce a colour that will darken surfaces and others, like white polish are colourless. Shellac has many uses. It is the main ingredient in French polish which is applied over hard woods with a 'rubber' or cotton wool pad to produce a super-fine finish and deep shine. It can also be used as a binder in which to suspend colour and solvent. Home-made lacquer paints (see page 114) can be created by mixing white polish with pure pigments dissolved in methy-

Wax/Varnish/Lacquer	Type and use
Beeswax	Soft, white wax from honeycombs. Can be softened with heat and mixed with pigments or artist's oil colours to stain wood or create specialist effects; also used for distressing effects.
Carnauba wax	One of the hardest waxes available; dark brown, can polish up to a very high shine for woodwork. Very high melting point. Comes from the Brazilian palm.
Liming wax	White wax; chalk (whiting) or white pigment is added to produce liming and antiquing effects for hard woods, e.g. oak and ash.
Boot polish	Very versatile, household product. Ideal for polishing and antiquing freshly painted surfaces. Wide colour range.
Polyurethane varnish (matt, satin, gloss)	The most widely available of oil-based varnishes. Clear with a slight yellowing tinge. Slow drying, tough. Darkens over time.
Yacht varnish	Extra-tough, high resistance to water and wear and tear. Yellows.
Acrylic varnish (matt, satin, gloss)	Water-based. White, opaque, with a pearly shimmer when wet; dries transparent. Matt is rarely completely flat. Extremely quick drying but does not achieve as smooth, flexible or hard-wearing a finish as oil-based varnishes.
Crackle glaze (crackle varnish)	Water-based. Causes water-based paints to split and reveal the surface underneath (see page 84).
Craquelure	Two varnishes of different drying speeds that react to produce a cracked effect. Traditionally a water-based varnish was applied over an oil-based one; complete water-based versions are now available (see page 84).
Gilding size	Slow-drying oil-based varnish that remains 'open' and tacky for application of metal leaf. Water-based versions now available are more flexible, but not suited for exterior use.
Shellac (white polish, button polish, French polish, black polish, knotting)	Fast-drying, alcohol-based resinous varnish. Can be applied in multiple layers and sanded to super-fine, lacquer-like sheen; used as binder for pigments and bronze powders. Heating produces different shades. Derived from the 'lac' beetle.

lated spirits, and gilders use shellac to seal metal leaf, a cheaper version of gold or silver leaf, and prevent it tarnishing.

Shellac can also be used to make rich metallic paints, as in our recipe on page 52 where white polish is combined with metallic powders. Confusingly called 'bronze powders' these come in many different shades: bronze, copper, gold, silver, etc. They are obtained from metals like copper, zinc and aluminium and, because these are less pure than precious metals like gold and silver, will eventually oxidize and tarnish if left unsealed.

MIXING PAINTS AND GLAZES

Always follow certain steps when you make your own paints or glazes or doctor ready-mades. Ingredients must added in a specific order – never put them straight into a receptacle and simply mix them together. Some materials are denser than others and must be broken up before they are added to the others. Some, particularly colouring agents, may need continual testing and should be added little by little until the desired shade has been achieved. The best order to follow is to put all the binder into a container and then add the tinting agent, a drop at a time. Pure pigments should be soaked in the relevant solvent beforehand and 'mashed'. Use a fitch (see page 36) to do this as its generous head of stiff bristles makes it strong enough to break up the ingredients and work them together. Artist's oils or acrylics must also be diluted in solvent to ease the distribution of the tinting agent throughout the binder and prevent lumps or streaks of pure colour. Then add the solvent to the binder until the correct consistency has been achieved. Add it very carefully or you risk making the mixture too dilute and having to start all over again, adding more binder and colouring agent, and probably ending up with too much paint.

SOLVING PROBLEMS

Most problems are caused by using ingredients in the wrong proportions. Others may arise if the underlying surface is badly prepared or painted with an unidentifiable material. For instance, a solution may 'ciss' – bubble or curdle as a result of contracting on the surface. This is why it is so important that you get to know your ingredients and the way they react to each other before embarking on too ambitious a project. Once you have this knowledge you will be able to call on a whole host of tricks and rectify a problem in minutes. In the case of 'cissing' you will discover that adding washing-up liquid to the solution reduces its surface tension and allows it to adhere to the substrate. Other tricks include neutralizing corrosive solutions on freshly stripped furniture by scrubbing with hot water and detergent before paint-

Problem	Cause	Solution
Paint or glaze is difficult to manipulate; dries too quickly, brushmarks stay	Not enough solvent. Hot weather. Application too thin. Too much drier	Increase percentage of solvent
Paint or glaze dries too slowly; does not adhere to surface	Not enough binder. Too much solvent.Cool weather. High humidity. Application too thick	Increase percentage of binder: (scumble glazes in case of glazes)
Water-based glaze will not adhere to an oil-based surface	Oil-based surface is not absorbent enough	Give surface a key by sanding and add PVA or washing-up liquid to the glaze; or sand and seal with shellac beforehand.
Mixture 'cisses'	Surface unabsorbent or surface tension too high	See above
Oil-based glaze won't 'settle' on a surface before being manipulated into a special effect	Badly prepared or uneven surface	Wipe the surface with linseed oil beforehand

ing, and adding whiting to a mixture to increase its opacity or PVA to a water-based wash to make it adhere to a vertical surface without running… The list is endless, but the table on page 33 will show you a few tips for some common problems.

BRUSHES AND TOOLS

Never economize when it comes to brushes. If any investment is to be made, it is here. If a brush is inappropriate, of inferior quality or in bad condition the finish

can be greatly affected. It is not always essential to buy the precise one that is recommended for a technique – some brushes can be adapted – but it is important to appreciate the different types available and their uses. There are some that it is wise to have in your tool box. Regular decorator's brushes, ranging in size from 1 inch (2.5cm) to 4 inches (10cm), are useful for priming and for applying most household paints, both oils and emulsions. Good-quality varnish brushes with natural, hog hair bristles enable you to apply varnish smoothly and are also useful for applying glazes. Use 1–2 inch (2.5–5cm) ones for small objects, 4 inch (10cm) ones for larger areas. Stencil brushes should also be natural bristle and cut to a domed end for skilful stencilling and subtle shaded effects. A hog hair softener or dusting brush is essential for colourwash effects; the softer the bristles the more cloudy the effect. Badger hair versions are the kings of softeners with their extra-soft bristles. They are ideal for sophisticated scumble glaze effects like marbling and graining but very expensive. Fitches are invaluable for mixing paints and glazes: their densely packed heads of long, stiff bristles are perfect for breaking up ingredients like raw pigments and artist's colours. Dragging brushes, made of stiff, wiry, horse hair bristles, are excellent for woodgraining as well as for dragged glaze effects. A large selection of artist's brushes is always recommended for hand-painting and other fine decorative work. Sable, camel and squirrel hair are all of proven quality and longevity.

Above all, look after your brushes. The more care they receive, the longer they will last. I have known some decorators hang on to a favourite one for years. A brush should always be cleaned immediately after use, not left for later. Make sure the particles of paint are removed from its stock, the point at which the bristles are held together and attached to the handle. It is easy to miss this. Never let the stock sit in white spirit, thinner or any other solvent-based solution when you soak brushes: the liquid can sometimes dissolve the glue binding the bristles and handle. Brushes used for oil-based techniques must be washed in white spirit, rinsed with hot water and detergent and then conditioned with hair-conditioner or brush-restorer.

Overleaf you will see various brushes and their purposes explained. The photograph on pages 38–39 is of other decorative equipment and materials. Get to know all of them. Most are required for the techniques in Sections Two to Five and the others will definitely come in handy at some point.

Brushes and other equipment

1 Chisel fitch
for cutting-in

2, 3 Flat end brushes
for furniture painting

4 Rubber rocker
for wood graining

5 Wire brush
for clearing wood grain
for liming

6 Stencil brushes

7 Decorator's brushes
for emulsions and other
paints

8 Fitches
for mixing paints and
glazes

9 Goose feather
for marbling

10 Badger hair softener
for softening oil glazes

11 Sea sponge
for sponging 'on' and 'off'

12 Pencil over-grainer
for woodgraining

13 Steel comb
for combing and
woodgraining

14 Stippling block
for stippling glazes

**15 Gilder's varnish
brushes**

16 Hog hair softener
for colourwashing

17 Horse hair 'flogger'
for woodgraining

18 Synthetic sponge
for applying colourwash

19 Over-grainer
for woodgraining

20 Soft mop-head brush
for gilding

21 Sword-liner
for freehand lining

22 Artist's brushes
for fine art and details

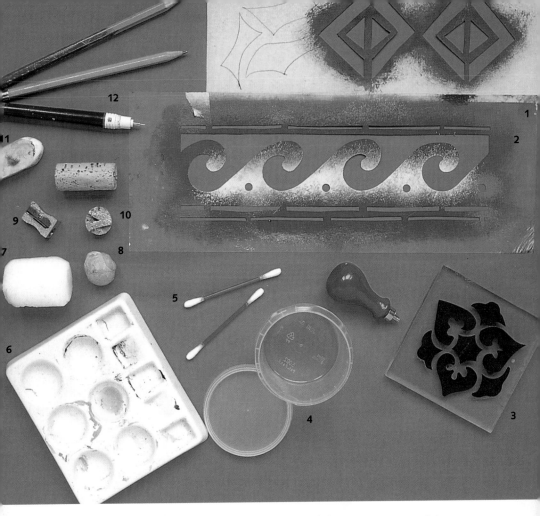

Decorating tools and materials

1 Oiled stencil card
for cutting your own stencils

2 Acetate
for cutting stencils

3 Rubber sponge stamps
for stamping effects

4 Pots and jars
are useful for many purposes

5 Cotton buds or swabs
are useful for tidying up
hand-painted work

6 Artist's palette

7 Candle wax
for distressing techniques

8 Plasticine
for vinegar graining
effects

9 Pencil sharpener

10 Corks
for stamping effects

11 Eraser

12 Pencils and pens

1 Transtrace paper
for tracing designs onto furniture and stencils

2 Ready-printed furniture patterns – useful for beginners

3 Photocopied motifs
are ideal for decoupage

4 Scissors,
the sharper the better

5 Steel ruler
(wood can get cut when using craft knives)

6 Tin opener
for opening stubborn paint lids

7 Craft knife
for stencil-cutting

8 Lining tape
for achieving straight lines

9 Masking tape
to secure stencils etc.

10 Sandpaper
for preparation and distressing new paintwork

11 Steel wool
for distressing fresh paint work

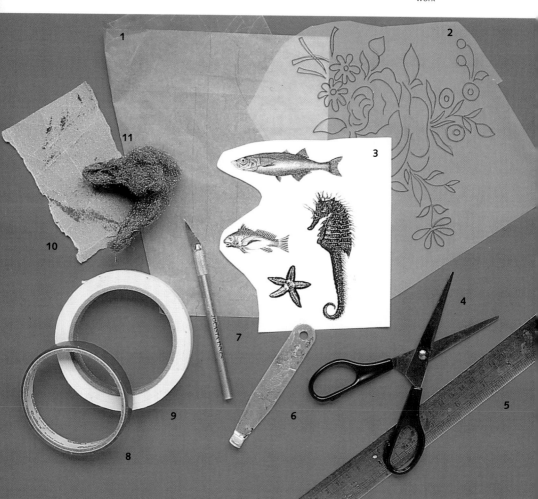

PLANNING AND PREPARATION

The more planning and preparation you put into your project, the more enjoyable and successful it will be. Here are a few pointers:

Paint coverage

Acrylic primer/undercoat	160–170sq. ft (15–16sq. m) per quart (1 litre)
Oil-based undercoat	160sq. ft (15sq. m) per quart (1 litre)
Matt emulsion	150sq. ft (14sq. m) per quart (1 litre)
Vinyl silk emulsion	160sq. ft (15sq. m) per quart (1 litre)
Oil-based eggshell	160sq. ft (15sq. m) per quart (1 litre)
Oil-based gloss	180sq. ft (17 sq. m) per quart (1 litre)

1 Make sure you have set aside enough time for mixing and experimenting. It is a common mistake to think that a process is quick and easy. It is not, particularly when you are dealing with colour. It takes time to get proportions and tones exactly right. Don't rush it.

2 Make sure all ingredients and equipment are immediately to hand. Read the recipe fully or you may miss certain items which could make the exercise a waste of time as well as money. Make a complete list of what you will need and tick items off as you get them. Newspapers and rags are always useful, as are lots of containers like jam jars and bowls for mixing solutions.

3 Work out how much paint or glaze you will need before you start to mix it. An obvious point, but it is all too easy to run out of a mixture in the middle of a project. It is difficult to re-mix an exact shade or consistency and you may waste valuable ingredients trying to do so. The amount of paint or glaze will depend on the area of the surface, but will also be affected by its absorbency and the thickness of the paint itself. Dilute materials go a lot further than thicker, more textured ones. The underlying surface will absorb and 'drink' up more paint if it is particularly porous or badly prepared.

4 Always check the manufacturer's instructions. Some materials are highly toxic. Work in well-ventilated areas if you are using oil-based products. You will spend some time working with the ingredients and and it is easy to be unaware that you are inhaling fumes, which can leave you with a nasty headache. Never sleep in a freshly painted room until it has been well ventilated. Do not smoke near flammable products and be careful to soak rags used to wipe up oil-based products in water. Always remove them from the house as they are known to self-combust in confined spaces like plastic bags.

5 Test the paint or glaze as you go. Cover pieces of card or wood with the base-coat colour and check the effect when your chosen shade is applied. If you are trying to mix the right colour for your project,

or create a particular effect, apply it to large pieces of card (painted with your chosen base coat, if necessary) and live with them for a few days before committing yourself. Put the cards in different positions in your room and see how the light affects the colour or decorative treatment throughout the day. Hold the card up to other colours or objects in the room to see how they sit together.

6 Be armed with plenty of solvent – water, white spirit or methylated spirits – to remove mistakes. Use hot water and a scourer to remove freshly applied water-based paints and cotton rags soaked in white spirit for oil-based ones. Always use clean equipment: I have known buckets of valuable materials to be wasted because small amounts of tinting agent were left in the bristles of a mixing brush. Clean brushes in warm water with a bristle scrubbing-brush, and

work from the stock down. Professionals use *Savon de Marseille*, an olive-oil-based soap, to clean and condition bristles. In our projects we give you the choice of using separate brushes for different steps or simply using well-cleaned ones.

7 If you have changed or added to a recipe remember to write down the ingredients and proportions. If you want to make up more of the paint or glaze at a later date, or have to repair the finish, you will need a detailed record of how you mixed it.

8 Store mixed paints in airtight containers if you want to preserve them. Don't put oil-based paints or glazes in plastic as this will eventually melt. In fact, they will not last much more than a month without separating and drying out. Water-based ones contain large quantities of bactericide to preserve them and will last a long time in airtight conditions.

8 CLASSIC RECIPES FOR THE HOME DECORATOR

This section contains seven
essential paint recipes for home
decorators: a wall paint, woodwork
paint, lacquer paint, metallic paint,
a classic scumble glaze, an antiquing
patina and an antiquing wax.
Between them they use the full range
of binders, tinting agents and
solvents discussed earlier. Once
you have mastered these classic
recipes you will be well-equipped to
take on most decorative projects.

43

DISTEMPER A traditional, water-based wall paint, distemper is subtly textured with a rich, chalky matt finish, soft on the eye and soft to the touch, and has an exceptional bloom when tinted to pretty pastels. A lot of pigment is required to colour it, so it is best to stick to paler shades. Distemper can be applied over most paints, plasters, and even wall- or lining paper. Any left over may be stored in a refrigerator for a few days but will then 'go off' because of its organic content.

CLASSIC RECIPE
8lb (3.5kg) whiting
pure pigment (for the colour of your choice)
4oz (113g) rabbit skin glue granules

1 Fill a deep paint kettle or bucket with water and pour in the whiting until just a peak shows above the water-line. Leave to soak overnight, then use a whisk to break up any lumps. If the distemper is to be tinted the pigment must also be soaked overnight. Put in a container with just enough water to cover. This helps to soften grittier colours and makes it easier to mix them into the whiting mixture.

2 Heat $^3/_4$ pint (450ml) water in a double boiler then add the rabbit skin glue granules a little at a time. Keep the glue at a medium temperature until it has melted completely. Let cool until tepid. Stir the whiting and water mixture, then add the glue to it, little by little. Continue stirring until you are sure the glue is evenly distributed throughout the medium.

EQUIPMENT
For mixing distemper:
deep paint kettle or bucket
whisk
container for soaking
  pigment
double boiler
fitch(es) for whiting
  and pigment
pieces of card
sieve
For applying distemper:
4 inch (10cm) decorator's
  brush

INGREDIENTS
whiting
pure pigment
rabbit skin glue granules

3 Add the soaked pigment to the distemper, bit by bit, until the desired shade has been achieved. Test the colour on pieces of card throughout this process (a hairdryer will speed this up) and remember that distemper dries at least 50 per cent lighter than the shade it is when wet. Remove any lumps by pushing the mixture through a sieve.

4 Apply the distemper to the prepared wall. Work the paint onto the wall in thick, horizontal brush strokes. If there are lumpy patches brush them out vigorously with the brush, first horizontally and then vertically. Remember, however, that some texture is very much part of the look.

COLOURWASH Distemper can look very pretty as a wash. Diluted with water and applied thinly over a base of untinted distemper, it produces a dappled, tinted look, with patches of the base showing through. This is an economical way of using pigment, as only the wash is tinted and not the initial base coat.

1

2 Apply a second wash of tinted distemper and this time fill in the white patches. As it dries there will be a subtle variation between the different patches, producing a colourwashed appearance of great softness.

2

1 Apply a solid coat of white distemper with a 4 inch (10cm) decorator's brush and leave to dry completely for 24 hours. Tint the remaining distemper with pigment and then dilute it with enough water to make a fluid, milky thin wash. Apply the wash with a clean decorator's brush or a softening brush. Use crosshatching strokes and apply loosely so that some white patches show through. Allow to dry for at least 3 hours, or until touch-dry.

OIL PAINT Oil paints are tougher and more durable than water-based products and are ideal for areas like doors and skirting or base-boards that need protection from wear and tear. The simplest recipe combines linseed oil, pigment and white spirit. We have added boiled linseed oil to speed up the drying process. It is impossible to give exact proportions of oil to pigment because some pigments absorb more oil than others. A basic guide is 1 part pigment to 1 part boiled linseed oil and 1 part raw linseed oil.

CLASSIC RECIPE
500ml boiled linseed oil
500ml raw linseed oil
400g pure pigments in a colour of choice
500ml turpentine or white spirit

1 Pour some boiled linseed oil into a glass bowl and swirl it around until the sides of the bowl are coated. Add the pigment, a spoonful at a time, and dribble in more boiled linseed oil. Stir with a wooden spoon while you do this and continue adding, dribbling and stirring until a thick paste forms. This should be heavy and stiff enough to full off the spoon slowly. Add enough raw linseed oil to make the mixture flow more easily. Its consistency should be similar to that of double cream. Continue to stir while you do this to ensure that the pigment is absorbed.

2 Now add the white spirit – the solvent. Pour it in, a little at a time, until the mixture becomes a little thinner. Test its consistency on a piece of card or wood. Be careful not to make the mixture too dilute.

EQUIPMENT

For making oil paint:
glass bowl
wooden spoon
piece of card or wood
muslin, cheesecloth or old
  panty hose
paint kettle
fitch

For applying oil paint:
decorator's or varnish
  brush(es)

INGREDIENTS

boiled linseed oil
pure pigment (for the
  colour of your choice)
raw linseed oil
white spirit

3 The mixture must be strained to make sure any grit is removed. Place the muslin, cheesecloth or old panty hose over a clean paint kettle and push the paint through with the wooden spoon. Stir the mixture with a fitch.

4 Apply the paint to your chosen surface. Brush it out in all directions to achieve good coverage (this is particularly important if the surface is at all uneven). Now use a clean brush to brush the paint out more finely and create a smooth finish.

LACQUER Shellac – the material used most commonly in the West to imitate oriental lacquer work – is combined with pure pigment to make a shiny, protective coating that can be used for decorative effects or built up in layers to create a rich, deep polished surface. The first layers of tinted shellac should be more pigmented than subsequent ones; transparent layers over opaque colour create a more subtle effect than multiple layers of dense colour. Always prepare your surface well when using lacquer paint. An undercoat of an oil-based paint, well rubbed down for smoothness, makes the most satisfactory base. We combined a typically oriental rich red pigment with white polish for our clock.

1 Pour white polish into a small bowl and slowly add pigment, a little at a time. Stir the pigment and shellac thoroughly with a fitch, making sure there are no lumps or grit. If the mixture is gritty you can smooth it with a pestle and mortar or soak it overnight in a little white polish. The mixture must be the consistency of single cream. Add a teaspoon or so of methylated spirits if it is too thick

2 'Float' the lacquer onto your prepared surface. Paint in one direction only and flood the surface for a smooth finish rather than brushing it backwards and forwards – the varnish is quick drying and brushmarks will form if you keep on brushing it out. Leave for several hours to dry and harden. Do not sand this coat down as the process will affect the pigment content and diminish its colouring power.

3 Apply a coat of clear, untinted white polish with a clean brush. This will seal in and protect the pigmented layer. Allow this to dry and harden, then sand with fine sandpaper. Repeat Steps 2 and 3: a pigmented layer followed by a clear layer. Then finish off with several clear layers; allow each one to dry before applying the next.

EQUIPMENT

For making lacquer:
equipment for mixing white polish and pigment
fitch
pestle and mortar (optional)

For applying lacquer:
soft-bristled (ideally badger or squirrel hair)
flat-ended varnish brush(es)
fine sandpaper

INGREDIENTS
white polish
pure pigment (we used red oxide, burnt umber)
methylated spirits

METALLIC PAINT Metallic paints are used to create shimmering, decorative finishes to add texture and highlight details. Their rich consistency also makes them ideal for lettering and other fine work that needs to hold its shape. Few of the wide range of commercial products available have the true glint of metal. It is easy to make your own with metallic powders. Confusingly called 'bronze powders', these come in copper, gold, silver, etc. as well as bronze and must be bound when they are applied as paint. White polish, PVA and acrylic varnish are all suitable binders. The latter two are very dense so require more powder and the resulting paint tends to look less 'sparkly'. Metallic paint bound with white polish dries very quickly.

1 Don your mask, then put your binder – white polish, PVA or acrylic varnish – in a container and gradually mix in your chosen bronze powder. Stir well with a fitch to distribute the powder evenly. Test the consistency of the mixture on a piece of paper or card. If it is transparent, or if the metallic colour is weak, add more powder.

2 Add the solvent: water if your medium is PVA or acrylic varnish; methylated spirits if it is white polish. Add it drop by drop. If you make the mixture too dilute you will have to start over again – and powders can be expensive.

3 Use a varnish brush to paint a large, flat surface and/or a finer brush for more decorative work. If you wish to seal the finish and protect it further, apply a coat of polyurethane varnish with a clean brush.

Note Metallic powders are ground to such consistency that they can easily become airborne. Always wear a mask when you use them.

CLASSIC RECIPE
white polish or PVA or acrylic varnish
bronze powders
water or methylated spirits
matt, satin or gloss polyurethane varnish, to seal (optional)

EQUIPMENT

To make metallic paint:
mask
equipment for mixing
   paint
fitch
piece of paper or card
To apply metallic paint:
varnish brush and/or fine
   brush for details
To finish (optional):
varnish brush

INGREDIENTS

white polish, PVA or
   acrylic varnish
bronze powders
methylated spirits

OIL SCUMBLE GLAZE Scumble glazes are transparent binders to which tinting agents and solvents are added, and are used for techniques that rely on a combination of different layers of colour or configurations to create a particular look. Traditionally, they were used to imitate precious materials like marble or exotic woods. The ratio of solvent to binder is greater than that in regular paints, and this produces their characteristic transparency and also retards their drying time so that complex specialist effects can be achieved. They can be water-based – acrylic versions are the most recent of many commercial products – but oil-based scumbles, like the one below,

are strongly recommended for *faux* finishes as they remain open longer and are more easily manipulated. Always apply the glaze to a smooth, non-absorbent surface or it will dry too quickly and be impossible to work with. It is generally brushed out thinly over a particular colour and then manipulated with specialist brushes or tools. The base coat remains visible, giving an illusion of depth. On the right you should be able to see, clockwise from top left, the effects created by stippling, ragging, dragging and sponging over a scumble glaze.

1 Pour some boiled linseed oil into a paint kettle. Dilute the tinting agent of your choice in a little white spirit. Pure pigment may have to be soaked overnight in white spirit if it is particularly gritty. Artist's oils must be diluted down to the consistency of single cream with white spirit. Mix the diluted colour into the linseed oil. Use a fitch and add the tint little by little, until you have created your chosen shade. Remember to go lightly with the colour – it is easier to add it than take it away. And always have some white oil-based under-coat at hand; this is very useful for 'knocking back' shades that are too intense and making them a little softer.

2 Add white spirit – the solvent. Do this slowly, about a tablespoon, or splash, at a time. Stir the mixture all the time with the fitch and check its consistency as you go. Apply it to card painted with your chosen base colour, then hold the card upright to see whether the glaze will adhere to its surface without running. And brush some of the glaze thinly on card and drag it, or press a rag into it, to see how well it holds a shape. If the the marking dissolves out you have used too much solvent and must add more medium – linseed oil. You should end up with roughly the same quantities of linseed oil and white spirit. If you wish, a very small amount of Terebine drier or siccative can be added to accelerate the drying process. Some painters add a spoonful of oil-based varnish too, to give body and strength.

EQUIPMENT

For making oil
scumble glaze:
paint kettle
fitch
tablespoon
card
cotton rags

INGREDIENTS

boiled linseed oil
artist's oil colours
white spirit
white oil-based undercoat
Terebine drier or siccative
polyurethane varnish
(optional)

CLASSIC RECIPE

50% boiled linseed oil
artist's oil colour, pure pigment or universal stainer
50% white spirit
white oil-based undercoat
Terebine drier or siccative (optional)

ANTIQUING PATINA Antiquing patina is a water-based glaze that lends instant age to freshly applied paint, disguises inferior materials or dubious handiwork and restores antiques. Simply tint a varnish – we used a matt acrylic one – with a 'dirtying' colour like raw umber or burnt umber and dilute it with a little solvent. Apply multiple coats, and wipe the wet finish back here and there, to achieve a deep, aged effect – dust and grime will collect in recessed areas but be polished off raised ones. For interest, our illustration also shows the effects of a ready-made patina and antiquing wax.

CLASSIC RECIPE
matt acrylic scumble
artist's acrylic colour: raw umber or burnt umber
water
matt or satin acrylic varnish, to finish

1 Pour the matt scumble into a clean paint kettle. Like most acrylic products it will look white and opaque, but will dry clear. Squirt some artist's colour into a small cup and add a small amount of water. Break up the colour with the fitch. Slowly add the water and paint mixture to the scumble until the desired intensity has been achieved. Check this on the coloured paper. The tinted varnish should not change its colour dramatically but should leave a thin, transparent glaze through which the shade underneath can be seen.

EQUIPMENT
To make antiquing patina:
paint kettle
small cup
fitch
piece of paper, the colour
  of your surface
To apply antiquing patina:
varnish brush
cotton rag
To finish: varnish brush

INGREDIENTS
matt acrylic varnish
artist's acrylic colour

2 Add water – the solvent – to the tinted varnish. The amount will depend on the use to which you will put the patina – you may need a thickish glaze if the surface is vertical or if a lot of moulding needs covering. We used 1 part water to 9 parts varnish. Apply the patina, brushing it out thinly, particularly if the surface is flat.

Gently press a cotton rag into the glaze to break up any obvious brushmarks. Leave to dry for about 30 minutes and then use a clean brush to apply a coat of untinted varnish.

COLOURWAX Colourwax is ideal for revitalizing furniture or floorboards or enriching colours if you do not have the time or materials for repainting or glazing. It will add depth and subtlety to hand-painted decoration and will achieve the gentle sheen of older pieces that normally only comes with time. A simple version is made by mixing raw pigment into softened beeswax. The pigment must be crushed very finely and dissolved in a little white spirit but the result is surprisingly effective. Keep any leftovers in a sealed jar for repolishing later.

EQUIPMENT
To make colourwax:
glass jar
saucepan of hot water or
  hair drier
fitch
fork
To apply colour wax:
soft steel wool
cotton rags

INGREDIENTS
beeswax
pure pigment (or the
  colour of your choice)
white spirit

1 Scoop some beeswax into a glass jar and put the jar into a saucepan of hot water. Leave until the wax has softened. Alternatively, blow a hair drier on a hot setting onto the wax.

2 Dissolve a small amount of pigment in enough white spirit to form a creamy paste. Stir the mixture well to make sure all the grains are broken up. Add the pigment, a little at a time, stirring well with a fitch. Use a fork if the wax is still stiff. Continue stirring until the pigment is distributed throughout the wax and an even colour has been achieved. Apply the colourwax to your surface with soft wire wool. Use pressure to push the wax into the grain of the wood or it will wipe off too easily. Leave to set for 10–15 minutes, then polish with a clean cotton rag. For a more dramatic result, leave the wax to harden overnight before buffing it up.

3 RECIPES TO TRANSFORM TILES, FABRICS AND FRESH PAINTWORK

It's always useful to be familiar with some 'remedy' techniques that allow you to transform existing surfaces without necessarily having to strip, paint over or discard them completely. These are quick and easy and should allow you to avoid costly replacements around the house.

TILES Tiles are so glossy, hard and unabsorbent that very few materials stick to them, or if they do they generally blister, flake or scratch off. Tile primer is a soft and flexible oil-based product that 'clings' to their surface. Its flexibility comes from its high level of solvent – white spirit – so it can take up to three days to dry. It is most commonly available in white so you may need to apply two coats over dark tiles. Once these have dried you can paint them with a colour. Use a simple stencil or stamped motif to add pattern.

MATERIALS	EQUIPMENT
hot water and detergent	old newspapers
methylated spirits	masking tape
tile primer	1¹/₂ inch (4cm)
white spirit	decorator's brush(es)
soap	for tile primer and
matt emulsion paints	paint
for top colour and	cutting-in brush
decorative motif	sandpaper
artist's acrylic colours for	rubber stamp
grout lines	small brush or roller
satin acrylic varnish	artist's small brush
	lining tape (optional)
	varnish brush

1 Dust the tiles with a cotton rag and wash them thoroughly with a scrubbing brush, hot water and detergent. Then use a clean cotton rag to polish them with methylated spirits so that the surface is completely dirt-free – make sure you remove built-up grime in the grouted areas. Mask off any areas that you do not want to paint with newspaper and masking tape.

2 Apply a thick coat of tile primer, brushing it out carefully over the entire surface, including the grout lines, to ensure an even coverage. Use the cutting-in brush to work up to any corners or edges. Allow 3 days for the primer to dry and harden. Protect the area from water while the primer dries.

3 When the primer is completely set and dry rub it lightly with sandpaper to create a key. Paint it over with matt emulsion as in Step 2. Leave to dry for about 1 hour, then apply a second coat. This will ensure that the tile primer is completely covered. Allow to dry for about 1 hour.

4 Now use the rubber stamp to apply a decorative motif to the tiles. You will need a steady hand for this but the result is immediate and the technique relatively quick and efficient.

5 Use a small roller or brush to apply your chosen matt emulsion colour to the stamp. Check the positioning of the stamp on each tile and then press down firmly. Test on newspaper as you go, and do not use a lot of paint or it will smudge. Mix the artist's acrylic colour to make a stoney colour – we used white, raw umber and a little yellow – and paint the grout lines back in with an artist's small brush. This will add extra authenticity to the finished effect. If you are not confident of doing this freehand, mask the lines off with masking or lining tape.

6 Apply 2 coats of satin acrylic varnish. Allow the first coat to dry for about 20 minutes before adding the second.

FABRICS Water-based mediums can be mixed with paints to transform old, worn fabrics, giving them a new look that can have immediate impact on an interior. Patterns can be applied freehand, with stencils or with stamps and, once ironed on, are permanent and washable. Motifs from other decorative effects in a room can be converted into stencils to keep a theme going. Use fast-drying water-based paints like artist's acrylic colours, emulsion paints, poster colours or ready-mixed stencil paints. Our design was inspired by a motif in a pattern book featuring damask wallpapers of the seventeenth century.

MATERIALS
water-based fabric
  medium (we used Paint
  Magic's)
water-based stencil paint
  or artist's acrylic colour

EQUIPMENT
tracing paper and pencil
stencil card
stencil pattern (see page
  127)
craft knife
palette, plate or ceramic
  tile
fitch
stencil brush
old newspapers
masking tape
spray adhesive (optional)
damp sponge
hair drier (optional)
iron

Note To make a successful stencil, the motif must be converted into self-contained sections that can be easily cut out. Stencil card is impregnated with linseed oil to make it more waterproof, but for additional protection varnish it with an acrylic varnish before use. Although it does not last as long as other materials like acetate, it is easier to draw onto and to cut out.

1 Use tracing paper and a pencil to transfer your chosen design from its source onto a sheet of stencil card, then cut out the stencil with a craft knife.

2 Mix the fabric medium with your chosen colour in a 50:50 ratio. Do this on a palette, plate or ceramic tile and stir the materials together with a fitch to distribute them. Take a little of this fabric paint onto a stencil brush and work it through the bristles onto newspaper to ensure an even distribution of paint.

3 If your motif is particularly intricate, or if you want extra adhesion, apply a spray adhesive to the back of the stencil. This will also help to prevent paint leaking

underneath it. Position the stencil on the fabric and secure it in place with masking tape. Use the stencil brush to apply the paint in soft, circular movements, using less colour towards the middle of the motif if you want a shaded effect. Then peel the stencil away and begin the next motif. Always have a damp sponge at the ready to wipe paint off the back of the stencil.

4 When the fabric is stencilled leave it to dry for up to 1 hour. The drying time can be accelerated with a hair drier. Then iron the back of the fabric using a medium setting. This will fix the pattern and make it permanent and washable.

2

3

FRESH PAINTWORK Beer glazes have an unmatched delicacy and transparency that can be used to add subtle tints to freshly painted surfaces. They also dry more quickly than regular glazes, so are useful for mixing antiquing washes that can be quickly varnished over. Although most water-based paints can be used to tint beer, pure pigments in shades like burnt umber or raw umber are ideal. Mix the glaze in the proportions given below and apply multiple layers for darker, richer shades. For a more antiqued look, add extra pigment and a little sugar to make the glaze more sticky. This will also help it to adhere and settle in corners, recesses or mouldings.

MATERIALS
1 tablespoon pure
  pigment: raw umber or
  burnt umber
approx. 4fl oz (125ml) flat
  brown ale
matt or satin acrylic
  varnish

EQUIPMENT
cup or glass jar
fitch
piece of card
varnish brush(es) for
  glaze and varnish
cotton rag

2

1 Put the pigment in a cup or glass jar and add a little of the beer. Mash the two ingredients together with a fitch to break up the granules and distribute them evenly. When the pigment has dissolved add the rest of the beer, bit by bit and stirring all the time, until you have the shade and transparency you want. Test the mixture on a piece of card as you do this.

2 Paint the glaze onto your freshly painted surface. Apply it over the whole area, or in sections if the piece is large, and drag it in one direction using wide brush strokes to ensure even coverage. The glaze is quick drying, so brush out any strong streaks of colour as soon as they appear.

3

3 Wait for for the glaze to settle and dry partially – this will take 5–10 minutes – then wipe it back with a clean cotton rag. Wipe gently in all directions to achieve a subtle tint and naturally aged look. If too much glaze comes off it is too wet and another layer must be applied and left to dry partially. If you want a stronger effect simply repeat the process. For a more dramatic finish, allow the glaze to settle in corners or mouldings before wiping back. Leave it to dry completely, then use a clean brush to seal it with varnish.

5 RECIPES FOR
SUBTLE SURFACES

A selection of intriguing effects for
decorative objects and accessories.
Some include ageing techniques,
some tinted glazes, and some
ready-mixed 'special effect' paints;
all will bring a gentle sophistication
to the simplest of home objects.

SHAGREEN

The term 'shagreen' is of Turkish origin and refers to the finely granulated skin of sharks, used since the seventeenth century as a decorative covering for small ornaments like boxes, jewel cases or tea caddies. It was especially popular during the eighteenth century and enjoyed a revival during the art deco period when it was often used to cover larger pieces like designer tables and chairs. The effect was created by pounding moist, untanned sharkskin with seeds to give a pitting or granulated effect. The material was then colour-stained, usually a pale grey, green, pink or blue. Nowadays shagreen is a collector's item and craftsmen have formulated ways of imitating it with tinted glazes and specialist brushes. It is a surprisingly easy technique and an unusual alternative to the more common specialist glaze effects like ragging, sponging and marbling. Finishing touches such as gold or silver edging, or fine, hand-painted lines, add elegance.

MATERIALS	EQUIPMENT
primer	decorator's brush(es) for
oil-based undercoat	primer and undercoat
white oil-based eggshell	fine varnish brush(es)
paint	for base colour, glaze
white polish	and varnish
oil-based scumble glaze	wet and dry paper
white spirit	cotton wad or 'bob'
artist's oil colour	scouring pad
satin polyurethane	fitch and container for
varnish	mixing glaze
	stippling brush or large
	stencil brush
	cotton rag
	plant mister
	cotton buds or swabs

1 Prime and undercoat your object, and base-paint it with the white eggshell paint. Allow to dry. Smooth lightly with wet and dry paper, then apply a further coat of paint. Allow this to dry and then sand it as above. Apply a third coat of paint and leave it to dry. When this final coat has dried preserve or 'isolate' the finish by soaking a small wad of cotton in white polish and wiping the surface with straight, even strokes. Leave to dry, then scour off any ridges with a scouring pad. This will create an extra-smooth surface.

2 Now make up the glaze. Use 1 part white eggshell paint, 1 part oil-based scumble glaze and 1 part white spirit and stir well with a fitch. Add just enough artist's oil colour to tint the glaze to a pastel shade. Apply the glaze to the surface and brush it out thinly and evenly.

3 Use a stippling brush or large stencil brush to stipple out the brushmarks and create an all-over, finely speckled effect. If you have applied too much glaze – if it is not holding the stippled effect crisply – wipe it away with a cotton rag and apply a thinner coat.

3

4

4 Fill the plant mister with water and spray onto the wet glaze. This will force the glaze to open up, leaving the tiny, circular markings that characterize real shagreen. If the papillae-like dots do not appear immediately leave the object undisturbed overnight – they will open up as the water evaporates from the surface. If you are working on a vertical surface be careful not to spray too much water as it will run. For variation, accentuate some of the markings with a cotton bud or swab. Allow to dry completely for at least 24 hours, then use a clean brush to apply the varnish.

ANCIENT BRONZE

Wax normally provides a waterproof, protective coating for bare or painted wood, creating a soft sheen that can be polished and repolished. We have used it as a binder and tinted it with pure pigment and bronze powders to imitate the rich, dark brown tones of old bronze. Metallic effects are traditionally achieved with specialist paints and gilding materials or corrosive solutions that eat into the surface of a metal and distress it. These techniques are often fiddly or, in the case of corrosive materials, unpleasant to use. This recipe is quick and harmless and the results are tactile and sensuous. The wax will harden slowly once it has been applied and can then be buffed up.

MATERIALS	EQUIPMENT
black matt emulsion paint	brush for applying base
beeswax	colour
pure pigment: raw umber	glass jar
or burnt umber	saucepan of hot water or
white spirit	hair drier
copper metallic powder	fitch
	fork
	stencil brush
	cotton rag

2 Scoop some beeswax into a glass jar and put the jar into a saucepan of hot water. Leave until the wax is a soft paste. Alternatively, blow a hair drier on a hot setting onto the wax. Dissolve a small amount of pigment in enough white spirit to form a creamy paste. Stir the mixture well to make sure all the grains are broken up. Add the pigment to the wax, a little at a time, stirring well with a fitch. Use a fork if the wax is still stiff. Continue stirring until the pigment is evenly distributed throughout the wax and an even colour has been achieved. Repeat the process with the copper powder.

Note Water-based paints do not adhere satisfactorily to varnish or glossy paint. Make sure your object is clean and well sanded before you start.

1 Paint your object with the black paint and leave to dry for about 1 hour. Apply a second coat if the coverage is not even. This will provide the dark base colour required for the bronze effect.

3 Stipple the wax paste over the base colour with a stencil brush. There should be a thick covering of paste with just a little of the base colour peeping through here and there to provide variations in tone. Leave the wax to harden over 24 hours.

4 Polish and buff up the tinted wax with a clean cotton rag. This will create a rich, handsome sheen, with the metallic powders gleaming through the dark bronze tones. The effect should be polished occasionally and kept away from water. It must not be varnished.

3

4

PORCELAIN CRAQUELURE Craquelure is often confused with crackle glaze (see page 89) which causes one paint colour to crack over another. The term originates in France and describes a finish that imitates cracked, aged varnish. Because craquelure is transparent, it is usually applied over decorations like decoupage or hand-painted motifs to give an authentically antique look. The effect is based on a two-tiered system: when a thick, quick-drying varnish is applied over a thin, slow-drying one fine cracks appear on the surface. Artist's oil colour is rubbed into the cracks to accentuate them further. Traditionally, incompatible water- and oil-based varnishes were combined but reliably efficient and easy-to-use water-based systems are now available. Oil colours are used to emphasise the cracks as they remain workable and can be wiped away – acrylics would settle over the whole surface. Water-based craquelures must always be sealed with an oil-based varnish 24 hours after the oil colour in the cracks has dried hard. An unprotected finish will eventually blister and flake off, or dissolve when water touches it.

MATERIALS
matt emulsion paint
water-based craquelure
  (we used Paint Magic's)
artist's oil colour
white spirit
satin polyurethane varnish

EQUIPMENT
brush for applying base
  colour
varnish brush(es) for
  craquelure and varnish
cotton rags

2 Fine hair-line cracks will appear across the surface when the varnish has dried. Hold your object up to the light and check that the entire surface has cracked and not just some areas. Don't worry if you spot any smooth patches – the varnish may have been applied more thickly in those areas and just need more time to dry. Rub artist's oil colour into the cracks with a cotton rag or your fingers. The varnishes are transparent so the craquelure effect will be only be noticeable when the paint is applied.

1 Paint your object with matt emulsion paint and leave to dry. Apply a second coat to ensure opaque, smooth coverage. Allow to dry, then apply the thin, sticky varnish. Do this quickly to ensure an even application. Do not brush backwards and forwards too many times; if you do, the material will become difficult to manipulate. Leave to dry for 30–40 minutes, then apply the thicker varnish. You will have to brush it out with some force to achieve a smooth application. Dipping your brush into hot water first will help. Allow 2–3 hours for this second varnish coat to dry completely.

3 Remove excess oil colour with a a few
drops of white spirit and a cotton rag,
leaving just enough to fill the cracks with
colour, then buff up the surface with a
fresh cotton rag. The top varnish will be
slightly stained. Leave the colour to settle
and dry in the cracks for 24 hours then seal
the finish with the polyurethane varnish.

RICH 'LEATHER' Craftsmen have been using their skills to simulate the effects of age and wear since decorative finishes were invented but today all sorts of ready-to-go products are available. Crackle glaze is one of them and is used for a dramatically handsome antiqued effect. This thick, water-based medium creates the finish by causing one paint colour to crack over another, and is as easy to do as it is effective. It can only be combined with water-based paints and you must brush the top coat on liberally and quickly as it reacts immediately. Brush either backwards or forwards – if you do both you will interrupt the cracking process. If you apply the crackle glaze in one direction – north to south – and the top coat of paint across it – east to west – the cracks tend to be more dramatic. If you want large cracks, paint the top coat of colour on thickly, and give it a blast with a hair drier. We used the glaze to imitate old crocodile skin, an eminently suitable and classy disguise for our tin hatbox, but it can be used on a variety of objects from picture or mirror frames to blanket boxes and trunks.

MATERIALS	EQUIPMENT
2 tones of matt emulsion paint: 1 light, 1 dark	brush(es) for paints
water-based crackle glaze	varnish brush(es) for crackle glaze and
button polish	button polish
methylated spirits	cotton rag
boot polish to match the darker paint	

1 Apply the light base paint to your object, and leave to dry. Then brush on a thick coat of crackle glaze, working either backwards or forwards. If your surface is vertical brush the glaze out well to prevent 'sagging' or drips. Leave to dry completely – this will take 1–2 hours.

2 Apply your dark paint over the crackle glaze. It will begin to crack as soon as it touches the surface. Avoid rebrushing as this will interrupt the cracking process. Brush this top coat at right angles to the glaze for a dramatic, crocodile-skin effect. Remember that the thicker the top coat the bigger the cracks.

2

1

3 Apply two coats of button polish diluted with methylated spirits to produce the rich, glossy sheen of leather. This will also seal the effect and protect it from water.

4 Polish the surface with boot polish and buff it up with a cotton rag. This will knock back the glossiness of the button polish a little and give the finish a more waxy feel, similar to old leather.

VINEGAR GRAINING Vinegar graining is fun, bold and surprisingly effective and is suitable both for small objects and larger pieces like wardrobes and wooden chests. Because the glaze is sticky, patterns impressed on it will not dissolve out. It dries to a rather murky, matt finish, but once coated with shellac and varnished with a gloss varnish it leaps into glowing life. Mix the pigment, vinegar and sugar in the proportions given below. Traditionally putty, corks or fingers were used to make patterns. Plasticine is a good alternative. The best colours are woody shades like dark brown or rust red applied over lighter base colours like brick red or maize yellow. Make your patterns bold – the more movement, the more successful the final effect.

MATERIALS

vinyl silk or eggshell
emulsion paint
1 tablespoon pure
pigment
4fl oz (125ml) malt
vinegar
$1/_3$ teaspoon sugar
washing-up liquid
Plasticine or corks
button polish
gloss polyurethane
varnish

EQUIPMENT

brush for paint
equipment for mixing
glaze
varnish brush(es) for
glaze, shellac and
varnish

2 Roll a walnut-sized lump of Plasticine across the wet glaze (or use corks or your fingers). There is no need to create a specific pattern, although you may wish to experiment. This process makes wood-like markings by taking the colour off here and there to reveal the tone of the base coat. Do not leave any large areas of the glaze unmarked or the effect will be unbalanced. Leave to dry for about 45 minutes. Apply a coat of button polish to seal the effect and create a rich golden tone. Allow to dry for 10–15 minutes, then apply a protective coat of varnish.

1 Paint your object with emulsion paint and leave to dry. Dissolve the pure pigment in a little vinegar, then stir in the rest of the vinegar a little at a time until the mixture holds its shape – if it doesn't, add more pigment. Add the sugar, if you wish, to make the medium bind well. Continue stirring until the pigment and sugar are evenly distributed in the vinegar. Brush the glaze onto your surface with a varnishing brush or glider, dragging it to create even coverage. If the mixture 'cisses' – bubbles up and does not settle – a squirt of dishwashing liquid will reduce its surface tension. Brushing the glaze backwards and forwards will also help.

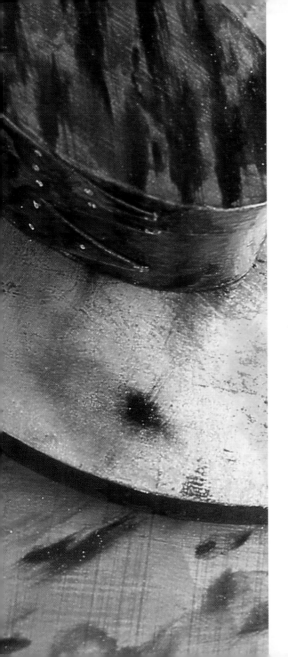

5 RECIPES FOR
GLAMOROUS EFFECTS

Spectacular, luscious effects,
most utilising gold and silver metal
leaf. Best suited to smaller, finer
pieces in your home, you will be able
to use them to add a touch of
richness to your interior, or even
create impressive gifts. Whatever you
try, you'll have fun.

FOSSIL STONE MARBLING To produce this *faux marbre* effect, two or three different-colour glazes are applied to a surface and spattered with solvents while they are still wet. Remember, though, that this is a technique for flat, horizontal surfaces like table tops or even floors – the solvent will run on a vertical one. Use soft umbers and siennas, greys and muted blues, and finish with several coats of gloss or satin polyurethane varnish. Mask off the surrounding area when spattering, and allow the solvents to dry for about 24 hours before varnishing.

MATERIALS
white oil-based eggshell paint
oil-based scumble glaze
white spirit
artist's oil colours
methylated spirits
gloss polyurethane varnish

EQUIPMENT
brush for paint
equipment for mixing glazes
1¹/₂ inch (4cm) varnish brush(es) for glaze and varnish
fitch for glaze
cotton rag or natural sponge
cup or glass jar
2–3 decorator's brushes or fitches for spattering
artist's fine watercolour brush or cotton bud/swabs

Note Smooth your surface with wet and dry paper before starting; and for an immaculate finish, follow the 'isolating' process in Step 1 on page 78.

1 2

1 Apply a coat of white paint to your prepared surface. Allow to dry for 24 hours. Mix 1 part oil-based scumble glaze and 2 parts white spirit in a bowl, then add your chosen artist's oil colour or colours a little at a time, stirring as you go. When you have achieved your desired shade, brush this first glaze onto your surface and spread it out thinly.

2 Make up a second glaze following the instructions in Step 1, but this time tint it with different oil colours to create a darker glaze. Use a fitch to dab this mixture over the first glaze in small, haphazard patches. Make some patches larger than others and make sure they are not too evenly spaced.

3 Now take a cotton rag or natural sponge and dab all over the wet glaze to break up brushmarks and hard edges. This will also help to take up some of the excess glaze. Don't worry if the two colours blend slightly – this will add to the final effect. For variation, twist the rag and roll it across the surface to form stone-like creases and folds in the glaze.

4 Pour a little white spirit into a cup or glass jar and dip a clean decorator's brush or fitch into it. Remove some of the liquid by tapping the brush against the cup or jar then spatter it onto the wet glaze. To do this, either bang the loaded brush against a clean one or flick its bristles with your thumb. Little holes will open out and

reveal the base colour as the white spirit settles on the wet glaze. Repeat the process with methylated spirits. This will create slightly different markings and add variety to the pattern. You can also spatter with water.

5 To accentuate the markings, use a fine watercolour brush or cotton bud/swab and white spirit to make some of the holes a little larger. Allow 24 hours for the solvent to evaporate and the glaze to dry completely, then apply a coat of polyurethane varnish.

RAISED GILDED WORK

Raised decoration was traditionally created with gesso, a thick, white water-based paste made of whiting (chalk) and water bound with rabbit skin glue. The ultimate primer, filler and texturing material, it can be sanded to a super-fine, marble-like finish – the reason why it has always been used underneath delicate water-gilding. Gesso can also be built up in multiple layers to create relief that can be gilded or painted. We have used a modern equivalent, acrylic modelling paste, which comes ready mixed and is quicker and rather easier to use. Like gesso, it can be shaped and then painted or gilded to create decorative effects on furniture, mouldings and picture and mirror frames. It is applied with fine artist's brushes and you will have to see yourself as a sculptor, using a brush to build up crisp, fluent shapes. The beauty of acrylic modelling paste is that it can be sanded, or even carved, and shapes can therefore be neatened up once it has dried. We used Dutch metal transfer leaf, which is cheaper than genuine gold leaf and certainly easier to work with, for our gilded decoration. We found the classical border in a traditional pattern book and transferred it to the frame with chalked transfer paper.

MATERIALS

acrylic primer
acrylic modelling paste
  (Liquitex)
red matt emulsion paint
water-based gilding size
Dutch metal
antiquing patina (see
  page 56) or dark brown
  boot polish
white polish

EQUIPMENT

brush(es) for primer and
  paint
chalked transfer paper or
  carbon paper (if
  transferring a design)
pencil
plate or ceramic tile
artist's fine watercolour
  brushes
cotton rag
scissors
finest grade steel wool
varnish brush(es) for
  white polish and varnish

1 Prime your object with acrylic primer. Use chalked transfer paper or carbon paper to transfer a printed pattern from a source book to its surface, or draw on your own freehand design. Use a sharp pencil to create crisp outlines that can be easily followed with the brush.

2 Spoon some of the acrylic modelling paste onto a plate or ceramic tile and add water, a little at a time, until the paste is smooth and the consistency of thick honey. Take a little paste onto the tip of a fine watercolour brush and fill in the pattern. Use the tips of the bristles to pull and sculpt the paste into shape. If the edges are rough or the surfaces uneven, dip the brush in water and smooth them out. You can really play with this material. If you are not pleased with the result wipe it off with a cotton rag and start again. You can add another coat to build up the pattern but allow the first application of paste to dry for 40–50 minutes before doing so. Leave this second layer to dry before going on to Step 3.

3 When all the built-up areas are dry apply a wash of red paint to the whole surface. Red clay or 'bole' was traditionally used over gesso and underneath gold leaf to add a rich tone to the metal.

4 Apply the water-based gilding size to all the areas that are to be gilded. It is white and opaque when wet but transparent when dry. Brush the size out thinly with a clean, fine brush and leave for 15–20 minutes until it is partially dry. Gilding size must be a little sticky or 'tacky', but not wet, for the metal leaf to adhere to it. Test the size with your finger: it should have the tackiness of masking tape. Use scissors to cut a sheet of Dutch metal to match one of the areas covered by gilding size and place it face down on the area. Rub over the backing sheet with your fingers or a brush and then peel it away. Press loose pieces of Dutch metal into place with a brush and brush away excess leaf.

5 Repeat the process in Step 4 until the entire surface is gilded. Gently rub back the surface with finest grade steel wool to distress it. Allow small areas of red to show through. Apply a coat of white polish to seal the effect and prevent tarnishing. If you wish to age your object further, apply an antiquing patina or rub it over with dark brown boot polish. Wait 10–15 minutes for the white polish layer to dry completely before doing so.

2 3
4 5

VERRE ÉGLOMISÉ

Although *verre églomisé* is named after the eighteenth-century art dealer Jean Baptiste Glomy, this truly beautiful finish dates back to Roman times when silver and gold leaf were applied directly to glass for a delicately shimmering effect. Further layers of glass were applied to protect the precious metal, creating a sandwich. It became fashionable to engrave the silver and gold leaf with intricate designs and glass decorated in this way was used to embellish burial chambers in the third and fourth centuries, to decorate Italian reliquaries in the early Renaissance and as inset panels on ornate furniture. This project by designer Alexandra de Zoete combines this traditional technique with a few modern tricks. She used etching acid and thick, oil-based stopping-out varnish – which produces a protective barrier against the acid – to produce wonderfully organic, freehand forms on the glass and then silver-leafed them to create an unusual lamp. Pure metal leaf is extremely delicate and beginners are often nervous when they handle it for the first time. You will find, though, that with practice you will learn to appreciate the quality and behaviour of this very special material – and there will be no stopping you.

MATERIALS
methylated spirits
stopping-out varnish
etching acid
warm water and detergent
white spirit
metal leaf (loose leaf)
fine-grade silicone carbide
   sandpaper
empty gelatine capsule
jam jar of hot boiled water
Vaseline
cellulose spray varnish

EQUIPMENT
cotton rags
pencil and paper
artist's brush(es) for
   stopping-out varnish
   and etching acid
mask and gloves
gilder's pad, knife and tip
varnish brush for size
cotton wool
very fine (grade 0000)
   steel wool

Note Etching acid can harm both you and your clothes. Wear a mask and gloves when working with it, and take care not to rub your eyes or get it onto your clothing.

1 Clean your glass thoroughly with methylated spirits and a cotton rag. Draw your pattern on paper with a sharp pencil, or trace it on using tracing paper, then lay it underneath the glass as a guide. Apply stopping-out varnish to areas that will not be etched.

2 Don your mask and gloves and apply etching acid to the exposed areas of glass. Leave overnight, then wash the acid away with warm water and detergent – remember to wear your mask and gloves. Remove the stopping-out varnish with white spirit and a cotton rag and clean the glass thoroughly with methylated spirits.

3 Fold out the protective paper guard on the gilding pad to prevent the metal leaf blowing away. Gently shake a single leaf at a time onto the pad and cut each one into 4 pieces with the gilder's knife. If the leaf sticks to the knife, de-grease it by wiping it gently with fine-grade silicone carbide sandpaper.

4 Dissolve half the gelatine capsule in a jam jar of hot, boiled water. Brush this size onto the glass. Tilt the glass as you do so to encourage the size to flow across its surface. The size will not stick to the etched areas. Use the gilder's tip to lay 1 piece of leaf at a time on the wet size. It will be easier to pick up the leaf if you rub a little Vaseline onto your hand and brush the gilder's tip over it to make the bristles a little sticky. Do not touch the leaf with

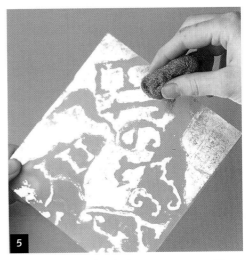

5

your fingers – the slightest pressure will make it disintegrate.

5 Cover the entire surface of the glass with leaf, then pat it gently with cotton wool to ensure adhesion. When dry, rub the surface with very fine steel wool to create a gently distressed finish and help to brush away any loose leaf. For variation, overlap small patches of gold leaf over the silver (or silver over gold) as shown. To do this, re-apply the size on selected areas and continue as in Step 4. These new patches can also be distressed.

6 Finally, seal the reverse (leaf) side with clear cellulose spray varnish (such as you would use on a car's bodywork). This is very important, as otherwise the metal leaf will tarnish.

TORTOISESHELL OVER GOLD LEAF There are a number of different ways of creating a tortoiseshell effect. We have used varnish stains rather than traditional scumble glazes, to give greater transparency and depth. And we have applied them over Dutch metal leaf, a departure from the norm that gives a very rich and sumptuous effect. Because the result is highly stylized, with exaggerated markings and strong directional movement, this technique is more suitable for small decorative objects like boxes, frames and trays than larger pieces. The key to the effect is to create the correct – tadpole-shaped – markings and to apply them fairly randomly; if the intervals between them are too regular you will end up with a spotty, leopard-skin effect rather than a tortoiseshell one. Softening is also important and it is essential to use a good-quality, soft-bristled brush – a badger hair softener is ideal – if you are to achieve the necessary depth, the 'tadpoles' should be transformed into sensuously blurred streaks that look as though they run through the very fibre of the 'shell'. Layers of tinted varnish submerge the markings further to make the effect all the more convincing.

MATERIALS
Dutch metal
gilding size
white polish
gloss polyurethane varnish
artist's oil colours: burnt
    sienna, burnt umber,
    ivory black
white spirit

EQUIPMENT
gilder's pad, knife and tip
varnish brush(es) for
    white polish, tinted
    varnish and gloss
    varnish
equipment for mixing
    tinted varnish
plate for mixing artist's
    colours
fine watercolour brushes
badger hair softener
sandpaper

2 Squeeze some burnt umber artist's oil colour onto a plate and mix with a little white spirit to make it more fluid. Use this to make tadpole-like markings in the wet varnish with an artist's fine brush. Make some shapes slightly larger than others, but ensure that they all run in the same direction – diagonally across the surface.

3 Repeat the process in Step 2 with ivory black, but make fewer, more delicate markings. You may want to use a finer brush. Allow the brush to 'trail' a little and taper off.

1 Gild your surface with Dutch metal following the instructions on page 104, then seal and protect it with a coat of white polish. Leave to dry for 10–15 minutes. Pour some gloss polyurethane varnish into a container and mix in enough burnt sienna oil colour to make a rich, golden shade. Dilute the mixture with 30 per cent of its volume of white spirit. Spread a thin coat of this tinted varnish evenly over the Dutch metal surface.

3

4

4 Soften using the very tips of the bristles of a badger hair softener. Follow the direction of the markings and 'tickle' the glaze to spread, lengthen and blur the shapes. Then brush across the markings to increase their width and blur them further. If you soften the shapes too much, add more markings, but make them thicker by adding less white spirit to the artist's oil colours, then soften again.

Allow 24 hours for the markings to dry completely then sand lightly. Mix polyurethane varnish with burnt sienna as in Step 1, but don't dilute; apply two coats to submerge the effect and give it more depth and authenticity. Leave to dry then sand again lightly. Seal with a final coat of polyurethane varnish.

ORIENTAL LACQUERWORK

ORIENTAL LACQUERWORK Genuine lacquer, made from the sap of the lac tree, is one of the world's most sumptuous finishes. Made up of multiple thinly applied layers – sometimes as many as 50 – and sanded at every stage, it is extremely hard, silky smooth and very durable. European craftsmen have been trying to imitate it since the first lacquerware was imported from the East in the sixteenth century. The most commonly used substitute is shellac which, treated in the same way as genuine lacquer, takes on its rich, glossy look. We used it to create this oriental-style box, but the effect can also be used on objects like small cabinets, trays, letter racks and picture frames. Craftsmen in the East carved into lacquer itself to create relief work and gesso was used to build up surfaces in the earliest Western imitations. We built up our motifs from a chinoiserie source book with acrylic modelling paste (see page 102) – a very satisfying contemporary alternative – and then gilded and lacquered them.

MATERIALS
matt emulsion paint
acrylic modelling paste
   (Liquitex)
water-based gilding size
Dutch metal (or see
   above)
artist's acrylic colours
button polish
methylated spirits

EQUIPMENT
brush for applying base
   coat
chalked transfer paper for
   tracing design
plate or ceramic tile
artist's fine brushes
medium-grade and
   super-fine sandpaper
scissors
equipment for mixing
   button polish and
   methylated spirits
varnish brush(es)

Note Bronze powder mixed with white polish is an easy-to-use substitute for Dutch metal (see page 53 for instructions) and can also be used to create a rich metallic paint if you want additional decoration on your object.

1 Paint your object with matt emulsion paint. If you are not creating your design freehand, transfer it onto your surface with chalked transfer paper.

2 Decide which areas of your design will be built up. They should be motifs that you want to come forward in terms of perspective. Do not choose any that are too intricate. Spoon some of the acrylic modelling paste onto a plate or ceramic tile and add water, a little at a time, until the paste is smooth and the consistency of thick honey. Take a little paste onto the tip of an artist's fine brush and fill in the areas to be raised. Apply a first layer and then build up, 'sculpting' the paste into shape with the tips of the bristles. Leave to dry for 40–50 minutes.

3 Apply more layers of paste – the number will depend on how much relief you want. Allow each layer to dry before applying the next one. When the final layer is completely dry, sand back lightly with medium-grade sandpaper. Apply the

gilding size to all the areas that are to be gilded and brush it out thinly with a clean, fine brush. Leave for 10–15 minutes until it is 'tacky' but not wet. Use scissors to cut a sheet of Dutch metal to match one of the areas covered by gilding size and place it face down on the area. Rub over the backing sheet with your fingers or a brush and then peel it away. Press loose pieces of Dutch metal into place with a brush and brush away excess leaf. Repeat this process until all the raised motifs are gilded.

4 Apply a thin coat of button polish to the gilded areas – this will help the paint to stick to them. Then use artist's acrylic colours and fine brushes to add decoration over these reliefs and other parts of the surface. Reds, green and blacks will maintain the oriental theme. Leave to dry.

5 Dilute 5 parts button polish with 1 part methylated spirits and 'float' it onto the surface. The material dries very quickly, so you should flood the surface with it rather than brushing it backwards and forwards. Leave to dry completely, then sand to a lacquer-like smoothness with super-fine sandpaper. Don't worry if the surface looks a little scratched – this will disappear when you apply the next coat. Continue this process until the raised work is buried under enough layers to hide any rough edges. The more coats you apply, the smoother and more luscious the surface will become – and the paintwork will take on a deep, golden tone.

2 3
4 5

GLOSSARY

Term	What it is	Purpose	Do's & don'ts
Acrylic colours	Artist's water-based paints. A huge range of strong bright colours plus metallic and pearlized finishes.	Tinting agent.	Cap tubes fast to prevent paint hardening.
Acrylic convertor (acrylic primer)	Water-based primer produced by Paint Magic, designed to adhere to oil-based paints. Matt finish.	For overpainting oil-based paint with water-based paint. Especially good on laminated surfaces such as melamine or Formica.	One coat will not cover, but will give good bonding for paint.
Acrylic primer	High-build paint with high degree of white pigment. Very opaque matt finish.	Covers bare wood, eliminating the need for an undercoat. Can be used as a cheap alternative to acrylic gesso.	Make sure surfaces are free of grease before applying primer. Rub down to smooth surface.
Antiquing patina	Water-based tinted wax.	Applied over freshly applied paint and selectively abraded when dry, it imitates natural wear and tear. Perfect for antiquing plaster objects.	Seal plaster objects with varnish before applying the patina.
Colourwash	Water-based transparent glaze or diluted emulsion. Some companies produce ready-mixed colourwashes, such as Paint Magic Colourwash, with an in-built retardant to slow drying time and enable easy application.	Creates a soft, matt 'fresco' look on walls. Can be wiped clean after full 'airing' time.	Allow 2–3 days before applying a second coat or varnish. Seal with varnish in bathrooms, kitchens and areas that will be wiped down.
Crackle glaze	Thick, water-activated glaze.	Causes one coat of paint to crack over another.	Use a water-based top coat, the thicker the better. Seal with an oil-based varnish.
Craquelure	A two-varnish system where a quick-drying varnish is applied over a slow-drying varnish causing the top one to crack. Artist's oil paint is rubbed into the cracks to colour them. Works particularly well over decoupage.	Creates an antiquing effect.	Make sure the entire surface is cracked before rubbing in oil colour. Allow 24 hours for the oil colour to settle and harden into the cracks before varnishing.
Decoupage	The application of prints or paper scraps to furniture or decorative objects.		

Term	What it is	Purpose	Do's & don'ts
Distemper	Traditional, water-based wall paint made from whiting, rabbit-skin glue and pigments. Allows walls to 'breathe'.	Creates a chalky, matt, velvety finish of great charm.	Mix carefully to avoid lumpiness. Do not varnish or overpaint with emulsion paint. Do not wash down. Discard any unused distemper as it is organic and will decay.
Distressing	Rubbing the surface of an object with steel wool or sandpaper.	Creates an aged effect.	
Dragging	Using a dragging or varnish brush close on a surface that has been given a layer of glaze and brushing it vertically or horizontally to leave fine stripes of glaze.	Creates a striped or strié effect on furniture and woodwork.	
Dry pigments	Naturally produced earth, mineral or vegetable powders.Concentrated and expensive but can be more economical than artist's colours.	Tinting agents for most paints, glazes and varnishes.	Pigments are highly concentrated, so protect clothing and add a little at a time when tinting.
Eggshell (acrylic)	Hardwearing and washable satin finish paint. Opague and non-absorbent. Quick-drying.	Use on woodwork and walls as a base for acrylic scumble glaze. Can be overpainted with oil scumbles if left to dry for a few days.	Apply quickly or brushmarks may show. Brush out smoothly with a fine brush.
Eggshell (oil-based)	Hardwearing and fully washable satin finish paint. Opaque and non-absorbent. Slow drying. Gives a fine, smooth surface with a slight sheen.	Suitable for furniture and interior woodwork. An excellent base for oil-based scumble glaze.	Work in a well-ventilated area.
Emulsion	Water-based paint. Can be tinted with universal stainers and acrylics. Matt (very opaque) or vinyl silk finishes. Absorbent, quick drying and washable. Silk emulsion less opaque but tougher and virtually non-absorbent.	Quickest, cheapest and fastest drying finish for walls and ceilings. Matt version can be used on new plaster. Can be diluted with water and used as a colour-wash if you are very fast with the paint brush.	Don't use vinyl silk emulsion on new plaster.
Fabric medium	Water-based, colourless medium that is mixed with paint.	Produces machine-washable paint for fabrics.	Flexible, non-bulky finish.
Gesso	Mixture of rabbit-skin glue and whiting (with hot water).	Traditional material used for filling cracks in furniture before gilding.	Sand down well between multiple layers for a smooth finish.

Term	What it is	Purpose	Do's & don'ts
Gilt creams	Metallic powders suspended in a turpentine-based wax to make a rich decorative material. Dries to a hard finish which can be buffed with a rag. Colours range from pale silver to deep, rich copper.	Perfect for metallic high-lights or touching up old gilded work.	Allow to set hard before varnishing.
Gloss (acrylic)	Hardwearing and fully washable paint. Non-absorbent. Quick drying.	Use as an alternative to oil-based gloss for interior and exterior woodwork.	Work quickly or brushmarks may show. Use nylon brush.
Gloss (oil-based)	Extra hardwearing and fully washable paint. High gloss finish. Slow drying.	Use on woodwork, particularly where a high degree of protection is required such as on exterior surfaces.	Work in a well-ventilated area and dispose of rags carefully.
Impasto	A thick, white, textured water-based paint produced by Paint Magic. Will cover anything and can be sanded smooth.	Creates effects from soft distressing to high-build textured finishes on walls and ceilings. Designed to be colourwashed to give a rustic finish.	The nearest thing to old distemper in appearance.
Knotting	Shellac-based material.	Seals resinous knots in new wood to prevent leaking sap staining paintwork.	Looks patchy, and should be painted over.
Lacquering	The application of multiple coats, originally of genuine lacquer but now more often of shellacs, varnishes or gloss paints, to a surface.	Creates a hard, smooth, shiny surface ideal for carving, gilding or inlay.	Prepare your surface well and apply lacquer very thinly, allowing each coat to harden before applying the next one.
Laminates	Tough surface materials formed by pressing together layers of different substances. Come in different forms such as Formica and melamine.	Most commonly used to clad kitchen units and countertops.	Rub down with steel wool pads before painting.
Limewash	Traditional paint made from slaked lime, pigment, animal glue and water. Allows walls to 'breathe' and does not peel and crack like plastic paints.	Use several coats on interior or exterior walls over porous surfaces, to build up a soft chalky bloom.	Do not apply over oil-based or vinyl silk paints, or other non-absorbent base paint.
Liming	Traditional, classic finish originally achieved with diluted limewash. A modern, tougher equivalent is white pigment mixed with beeswax. Some companies produce a paste version, e.g. Paint Magic Liming Paste.	Fills the grain of hard woods such as oak, ash and chestnut to create a silvery bleached look.	Take care not to inhale the dust produced when removing excess. Seal liming paste with shellac before applying varnish.

Term	What it is	Purpose	Do's & don'ts
Marbelizing	The imitation of marble with glazes and specialist brushes. Oil-based scumble glazes are most commonly used as they remain wet and therefore workable for some time.	Creates a faux marbre effect.	Mask off surrounding areas when applying glaze. Leave undisturbed for 24 hours before final varnishing.
Metallic powders	Made from copper, silver, aluminium or alloys.	Mix with shellac to make rich, lustrous metallic paints. Can be dusted over mediums before they dry to achieve a variety of striking effects.	Protect from oxidation with coats of shellac or varnish.
Methylated spirits	Unrefined alcohol. In Britain it is tinted purple, in the United States it is clear.	Solvent for spirit-based varnishes and shellacs. Can be used for stripping old shellacs or cleaning glass.	Work in a well-ventilated area.
Oil colours	Linseed oil and pigment. Soluble in white spirit. Slow drying. Cheaper student's range available, but artist's oils are more concentrated with finely ground pigments.	Along with universal stainers, the most convenient way of tinting oil-based paints and glazes.	
Oil-based paints	More flexible and durable than water-based paints, with a richer, more velvety texture. Slow drying. Eggshell and gloss finishes.	Most commonly used on woodwork, particularly soft woods like pine which require more protection than hard woods.	Make sure your work area is well ventilated. Soak used rags in warm water and remove them from the house. Do not leave in plastic bags.
Paint effects	See Distressing; Dragging; Lacquering; Marbelizing; Stippling.		
Primer (acrylic)	Water-based sealant designed to prepare the surface for another paint or varnish.	Use on new wood and old painted surfaces. Can be used for preparing laminates such as melamine and Formica for paint effects.	Make sure surfaces are free of grease and dirt.
PVA (polyvinyl acrylic)	Versatile adhesive medium.	Use as a sealer, binder or glue.	Test in thin solution first.
Scumble glaze	Transparent oil- or water-based medium into which colour and solvent are mixed to create glaze.	Use for techniques such as dragging, ragging, stippling, sponging, marbling and wood graining.	Make sure your surface is smooth and non-absorbent or the glaze will dry too quickly. Work in a well-ventilated area if you are using an oil-based glaze.

Term	What it is	Purpose	Do's & don'ts
Shellac	A quick-drying lacquer derived from shellac, an animal resin which is cleaned, crushed and dissolved in alcohol. Shellac is heated to produce darker shades such as french, garnet or button polish. Its solvent is methylated spirits.	Traditionally applied to stain and seal woodwork leaving a smooth surface. Can be used as a sealer for decorative work, or as a medium for metallic powders.	To avoid brushmarks, don't use an overloaded brush or overwork.
Solvent	Material used to dilute the main body of paint and tinting agent and make the mixture fluid and manageable. Also dissolves grime and old paint.	Creates transparency in glazes and extends their open or workable times. Use to wipe away mistakes and clean brushes and equipment.	Use turpentine or white spirit for alcohol-based lacquers and shellacs; water for water-based and acrylic products.
Stains	Oil-, spirit- or water-based substances.	Use to tint materials like wood or fabric, for a transparent finish.	Test on samples first for colour and absorbency.
Stamps	Rubber, cork, a potato or a synthetic household sponge, cut to create a raised decorative motif.	Use to apply patterns to walls, furniture, fabrics and other objects.	Apply paint to stamp with brush or roller.
Stencil paints	Rich, strongly pigmented water-based paints. Fast drying.	Stencilling on walls, furniture and fabrics.	Don't overload your brush when stencilling; keep it almost touch-dry to prevent bleeding under the stencil.
Stencil	A thin sheet of card or acetate in which a design has been cut.	Used to apply repeat patterns on walls, furniture, etc.	Don't overload your brush. Do wipe the back of the stencil regularly to prevent smudging.
Stippling	Decorative finish achieved by 'pouncing' the tips of bristles into wet glaze leaving pinpricks of colour.	Apply to flat surfaces such as walls and furniture.	Use light pressure, and stand back to gauge effect.
Turpentine	Liquid obtained from various coniferous trees. Paint thinner is a cheaper imitation.	The usual solvent for oil-based products.	
Undercoat (see primer)			

Term	What it is	Purpose	Do's & don'ts
Varnish (acrylic)	Milky looking varnish that dries clear. Gloss, satin and matt finishes. Quick drying and does not yellow with age.	Resistant, waterproof coating for painted and unpainted surfaces. Suitable for exterior work. Can be used as a binder in which to suspend colour and is useful for mixing quick antiquing glazes.	Stir thoroughly before applying.
Varnish (oil-based polyurethane)	Tough, smooth, hardwearing varnish. Gloss, satin and matt finishes. Slow drying. Slightly yellow and will yellow with age.	Particularly suitable for interior areas like kitchens and bathrooms that are subject to wear and tear.	Stir thoroughly before applying.
Verdigris	Paint effect that uses different shades of green emulsion stippled on with soft stencilling brush.	Imitates the patination of metals such as copper, bronze or brass caused by the corrosive action of air and sea water over time, which produces a green, powdery coating.	Don't finish with a gloss varnish, which kills the 'old' look.
Watercolours	Water-soluble transparent colours made from gum arabic and pigment.	Mainly used by artists for watercolour painting.	Must be sealed with shellac to preserve.
White spirit	A cheaper alternative to turpentine.	Solvent for oil-based products.	Don't inhale in a small space.
Whiting	Natural calcium carbonate ground to a fine powder.	Ingredient of gesso and traditional paints such as distemper.	
Woodwash	Thick, water-based paint manufactured by Paint Magic. Contains a thickener which allows it to be burnished once dry with wire wool and polished with antiquing or furniture wax to create a rich antique sheen.	Use on furniture as a transparent wash for new wood, as a rich opaque coat or to produce distressed finishes. (Matt emulsion can also be used.) Also suitable for stencilling and decorative hand painting.	Prime MDF with shellac before applying Woodwash (unnecessary on bare wood). Varnish areas that will be wiped down regularly.

SUPPLIERS

Specialist suppliers of traditional ingredients and brushes:

UNITED KINGDOM

Stuart Stevenson
68 Clerkenwell Road
London EC1M 5QA
tel (0171) 253 1693

Green & Stone
259 Kings Road
London SW3 5ER
tel (0171) 352 0837

A.S. Handover
Angel Yard
Highgate High Street
London N6 5JU
tel (0171) 359 4696

Cornelissen & Son
105 Great Russell Street
London WC1B 3RY
tel (0171) 636 1045

E. Ploton
273 Archway Road
London N6 5AA
tel (0181) 348 0315

Alec Tiranti
27 Warren Street
London W1P 5DG
tel (0171) 636 8565

UNITED STATES

H. Behlen & Bros
4715 State Highway 30
Amsterdam, NY 12010
tel (518) 843 1380

City Chemical
100 Hoboken Avenue
Jersey City, NJ 07310
tel (800) 248 2436

Restoration products, specialist varnishes, shellac and waxes:

John Myland
80 Norwood High Street
London SE27 9NW
tel (0181) 670 9161

Foxall & James
57 Farringdon Road
London EC1M 3JB
tel (0171) 405 0152

Liberon Waxes
Mountfield Industrial
Estate
Learoyd Road,
New Romney
Kent TN28 8XO
tel (01679) 67555

Craig & Rose
172 Leith Walk
Edinburgh EH6 5EB
tel (0131) 5541131

PAINT MAGIC SHOPS

Paint Magic offers a complete range of decorative paints, traditional ingredients, brushes, stencils and books. Each branch also offers weekly courses in decorative paint techniques.

PAINT MAGIC
MAIL ORDER
79 Shepperton Road
Islington, London
N1 3DF
United Kingdom
tel (0171) 226 4420
fax (0171) 226 7760

UNITED KINGDOM

PAINT MAGIC
ARUNDEL
26 The High Street
Arundel, West Sussex
BN18 9AB
tel (01903) 883653
fax (01903) 884367

PAINT MAGIC
BELFAST
59 The High Street
Holywood, County
Down BT18 9AQ
tel (01232) 421881
fax (01232) 421823

PAINT MAGIC
GUILDFORD
3 Chapel Street
Guildford, Surrey
GU1 3UH
tel (01483) 306072

PAINT MAGIC
ISLINGTON
34 Cross Street
Islington, London
N1 2BG
tel (0171) 359 4441
fax (0171) 359 1833

PAINT MAGIC
NOTTING HILL
5 Elgin Crescent
Notting Hill Gate,
London W11 2JA
tel (0171) 792 8012
fax (0171) 727 0207

PAINT MAGIC
RICHMOND
116 Sheen Road
Richmond, Surrey
TW9 1UR
tel (0181) 940 9799
fax (0181) 332 7503

UNITED STATES

Paint Magic products are stocked by Pottery Barn branches across the United States. For details of your nearest stockist, call Pottery Barn customer service (800) 922 9934, or write to:

POTTERY BARN
MAIL ORDER
DEPARTMENT
P.O. Box 7044
San Francisco, CA
94120-7044
tel (415) 983 9887

CANADA

PAINT MAGIC
CALGARY
101, 1019 # 17th Avenue
SW Calgary, Alberta
T2T 0A7
tel (403) 245 6866
fax (403) 244 2471

ISRAEL

PAINT MAGIC
TEL AVIV
255 Dijengoff Street
Tel Aviv 63117
tel (972) 3605 2476
fax (972) 3544 5710

SINGAPORE

PAINT MAGIC
SINGAPORE
Seik Yee Paint Shop
30 Watten Rise
Singapore 1128
tel (65) 463 1982
fax (65) 463 1982

FURTHER DETAILS

There are more Paint Magic shops opening worldwide in the near future. Please call or write for our catalogue, price list, Design and Decoration Service and details of the latest shop to open near you.

PAINT MAGIC
HEAD OFFICE
77 Shepperton Road
Islington, London
N1 3DF
United Kingdom
tel (44) (0)171 354 9696
fax (44) (0)171 226 7760

JOCASTA INNES AROUND THE HOUSE

If you have enjoyed using this book, you will also want to collect the other titles in this exciting new series. They are all available from good bookshops, Paint Magic, or by using the order form below.

COLOUR

Jocasta Innes believes that the short answer to mastering colour is that you learn by doing. With her wealth of experience, here are proven colour made simple. This pocket-sized book will give you control over and confidence with colour, and help you make it your friend and ally in making your home your own.

96 pages   colour photography throughout
£8.99 hardback
ISBN 0 333 71440 7

UNDERFOOT

Whether your problem is acres of dirty concrete or battered planks, here are innovative and stylish answers to your hard flooring needs. There is a wealth of tempting options underfoot, from glossed, crackled, stencilled, distressed or chequered paint, to stunning faux parquetry and floor tiles, and updates on traditional themes such as floor cloths and mosaics. Make the most of the riches beneath your feet!

96 pages   colour photography throughout
£8.99 hardback
ISBN 0 333 71438 5

IN YOUR OWN WRITE

Designer inspiration for your home! A room's decor is transformed by a stencilled motto, or the introduction of lettering as a motif, just as the impact of a gift is doubled by a personal dedication. Discover the fascinating world of lettering and how to use it as a design resource for fabrics, walls, furniture and accessories in stylish projects that encompass the contemporary and classical, and demonstrate the potency of writing as art.

96 pages   colour photography throughout
£8.99 hardback
ISBN 0 333 71441 5

Also available
THE NEW DECORATOR'S HANDBOOK
Jocasta Innes

A complete DIY decorating bible for decorating the Paint Magic way, with inspiration and practical techniques for transforming ordinary rooms, from the kitchen to the bedroom. Learn how to make strategies, understand how colour works and use the right equipment, paints and finishes, then follow the step-by-step guides for stunning effects.

192 pages   colour photography throughout
£15.99 hardback
ISBN 0 7522 1650 3

£12.99 paperback
available Autumn '97

ORDER FORM

Indicate the number of copies of each title required and fill in the form below.

Applicable only in the UK and BFPO addresses

Send to: **Macmillan C.S. Dept**
Macmillan Distribution Ltd
Houndmills Basingstoke RG21 2XS
or phone: **01256 302699**, quoting title, author and Credit Card number.
Please enclose remittance* to the value of the cover price plus: £1.00 for the first book plus 50p per copy for each additional book ordered.

*Payment may be made in sterling by UK personal cheque, postal order, sterling draft or international money order, made payable to Macmillan Distribution Ltd. Alternatively by Barclaycard/Access/Amex/Diners

While every effort is made to keep prices low, it is sometimes necessary to increase prices at short notice. Macmillan reserve the right to show on covers and charge new retail prices which may differ from those advertised in the text or elsewhere.

NAME AND ADDRESS IN BLOCK LETTERS PLEASE:

Name

Address

Card No.

Expiry Date

Signature:

1/97

STENCIL TEMPLATE

Use this stencil template, adapted from a traditional damask design, for the Fabric Remedy Recipe on pages 66-69. Either trace this outline directly from the book, or blow it up on a photocopier to your desired size. Use tracing paper and a pencil (or transtrace paper) to transfer it to a sheet of stencil card or acetate, and cut the design out with a sharp craft knife.

Stencil card is impregnated with linseed oil to make it more waterproof; for additional protection varnish with an acrylic-based varnish before use. Acetate will last longer, but card is easier to cut.

You may also want to adapt this to use as a motif with the Tile Remedy Recipe on pages 62-65, or one of the other projects in this book featuring stencils.

First published 1997 by Macmillan
an imprint of Macmillan Publishers Ltd
25 Eccleston Place, London SW1W 9NF
and Basingstoke

Associated companies throughout the world

ISBN 0 333 71439 3

9 8 7 6 5 4 3 2 1

A CIP catalogue record for this book is available from the British Library

Series Origination: Jocasta Innes
Text and Research: Sarah Delafield Cook

Design: Hammond Hammond

Original Photography:
Marie-Louise Avery, Sue Baker
Project Manager: Sarah Curran
Assistants: Sammy Dent, Tim Tari
Senior Commissioning Editor for
Boxtree/Macmillan: Gordon Scott Wise
Editor: Tessa Clark

PICTURE CREDITS
Marie-Louise Avery 1 (far left, second right), 2,
3, 5, 6 (top), 7, 9, 22, 41, 42-3, 44-5, 46-7, 48-9,
50-1, 52-3, 54-5, 56-7, 58-9, 60-1, 62-3, 64-5,
66, 68-9, 70-1, 72-3, 74, 75 (bottom), 77, 78-9,
80-1, 82-3, 84-5, 86-7, 90-1, 92, 94-5, 96 (except
bottom left), 97, 99, 100-101, 104-05, 111, 112-
13, 115, 116-17; Sue Baker 1 (second left, far
right), 6 (bottom), 10-11, 14, 17, 24-5, 28-9, 30,
34, 36-7, 38-9, 75 (top left), 93, 96 (bottom
left), 103, 107, 108-09; Paint Magic 124, 125

Scans and colour repro by Speedscan Ltd.

Printed in Italy by New Interlitho S.P.A. – Milan